CANAL CITY

Souvenir

Published by J.M.Pearson & Son (Publishers) Ltd., Tatenhill Common, Staffordshire DE13 9
Telephone/fax: 01283 713674 E Mail: JPEARSON@netcomuk.co
Web site: http://wwwpage.net.co.uk/pearsc
Print handling by Nexus Creative Print Services, Hall Green, Birmingham Tel: 0121 702 24
Publication of this book has been supported by British Waterways and part financ
by the European Community European Regional Development Fu

First edition 19
ISBN 0 907864 7

Acknowledgements

Grateful thanks from the author and publisher to: Mike Webb and Kevin Maslin for extra photographs; Graham Fisher for many a merry and eye-opening trip on *Diamond* and *Lady J*; to Jim Quinn of Birmingham City Council; Philip Calcutt of Birmingham Marketing Partnership; Tom Brock and Mel Bannister of British Waterways; and Steve Webb of Nexus. Cover photograph courtesy Birmingham Marketing Partnership.

Tamar Pearson

Hello,

"Where's your gondola?" asked the man on the roving bridge at Warwick Bar, with what I took to be the indigenous, caustic wit of the native Brummie. A subtle allusion to the frequently quoted claim that Birmingham has more canals than Venice, I assumed. Later, I chanced to catch my reflection in a shop window: straw hat, navy and white hooped T shirt, statutory black trousers; a pastiche gondolier, lacking only a neckerchief and a decent-size pole. It hadn't been humour, so much, as curiosity. The same sense of inquisitiveness which sends, on the surface of it, sane people - mostly, so far, middle-aged men of a solitary disposition - off to explore the canals of Birmingham and the Black Country: a hundred mile network of obsolete trade routes left metaphorically in the siding and the lorry park by quantum leaps in the technology of transport. This book urges you to join them, to find your way to Tipton and Dudley Port; Netherton and Brownhills. Canals are entering a new era, canals aren't freight anymore, canals are fun! I have no agenda other than the whetting of appetites. This is your illustrated menu. The choice of starter is yours.

Michael Pearson

Introduction

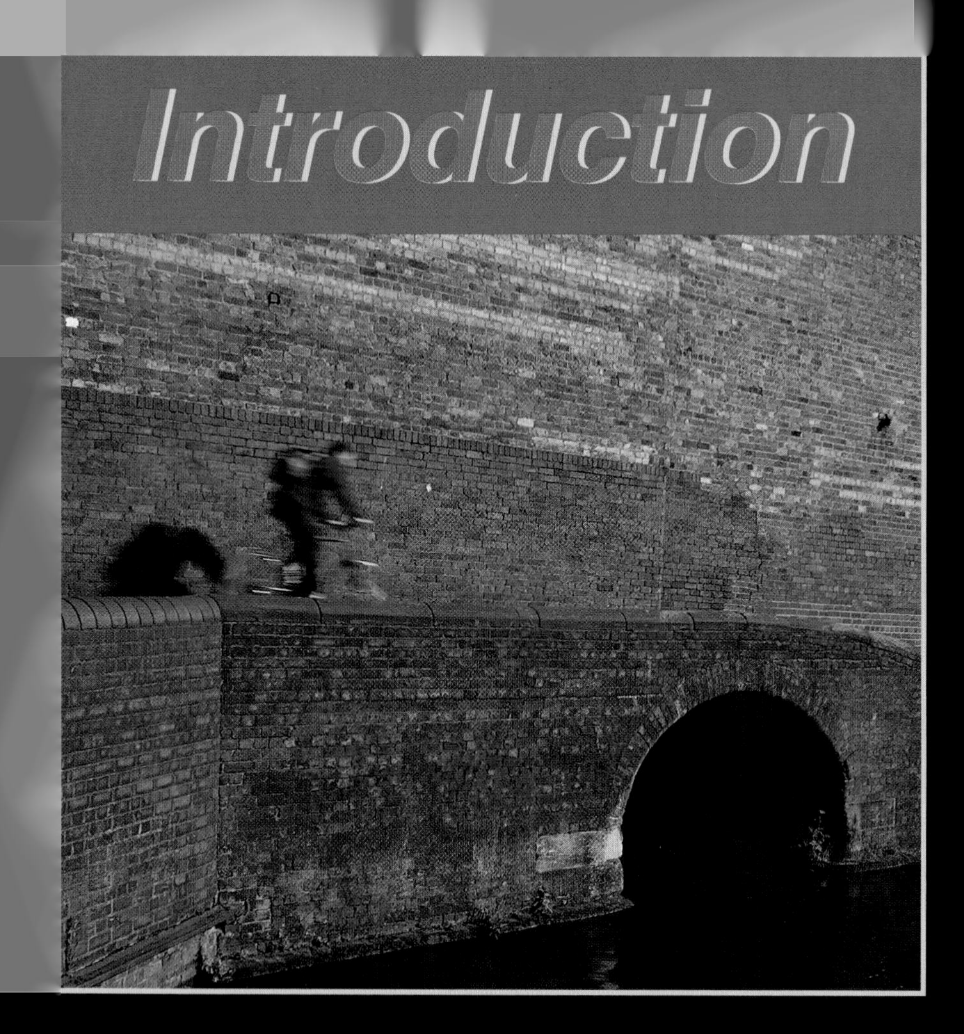

NO-ONE appreciates Birmingham's plateau top location more than the inland waterway boater. Long, energy-consuming ladders of locks lay obdurate obstacles in their watery path: Tardebigge from the south-west; Hatton and Knowle from the South; Curdworth, Minworth, Aston and Farmer's Bridge from the East; and 'The Twenty-One' from the North. All these arcane names strike dread into the heart of the canal traveller. There's no escaping them, nor the fact that Birmingham lies over 450ft above sea level, a not inconsiderable height in the context of the Midland plain.

Why were these waterways built at all? There must have been something worthwhile at the top of that hill. There was. It was coal. In North Staffordshire Josiah Wedgwood had hired James Brindley to build a canal to serve the pottery industry. At the other end of the county, and in neighbouring Warwickshire, it was Matthew Boulton, and other members of the Lunar Society, who sought out Brindl to build a canal to carry coal. By this time, around 1768, Brindley was a busy man, and though he surveyed the route, his assistants, Whitworth and Simcock - the Rozencrant and Guildenstern of the Canal Mania - were responsible for the day to day constructio of the canal. The first ten miles between Birmingham and the coal pits of Wednesbury opened in 1769 and were immediately profitable. The cost of coal in Birmingham was halved and the new canal attracted burgeoning industries to its banks, much as the nev Black Country spine road has created fresh industrial impetus between West Bromwicl and Walsall today. Within three years the canal had been extended to meet the Staffordsh & Worcestershire Canal on the far side of Wolverhampton, providing a total length of twenty-two miles including thirty-two locks.

Left: Modern day cyclists spare little time to think of the mysterious factory arms which once pass beneath the towpath.
Below: Leaning well over on the tiller to ease a boat off the Netherton Branch to join the main li at Dudley Port Junction.

Over the next hundred years the Birmingham Canal Navigations, as they became known, grew to a maximum extent of one hundred and sixty miles with over two hundred locks. They criss-crossed the plateau in a basket weave pattern, passing over and under each other, penetrating lengthy tunnels, sprouting branches and arms serving innumerable basins and wharves. It is no exaggeration to claim that the Black Country would not have soared to its industrial zenith without the canal network on its doorstep.

Providentially the Railway Age left them relatively unscathed. The new railway companies were happy to work in tandem with the existing canals. Transhipment depots were established at strategic points along the railways where cargoes would be transferred between canal boat and railway wagon to expedite delivery to, or consignment from, foundries and factories unconnected to the railway network. Similarly, the railways established 'boatage depots' along the canals for dealing with general goods.

Development of the Cannock coalfield boosted BCN tonnages in the middle of the 19th century. The Cannock Extension Canal of 1863 marked the last significant expansion of the system. It remained busy for a century with tug-hauled 'trains' of boats creating, quite literally, a tidal wave with their passing each day, bound for the power stations, blast furnaces and manufacturing plants of Birmingham, Walsall, Wolverhampton, Dudley and all their satellite communities.

Decline set in slowly, delayed by two world wars of petrol rationing on the one hand, and the commensurate effect that had on the growth of road transport, and increased trade on the other. Moreover, the Black Country has always been notoriously out of step with the march of Progress, and canal trade, particularly of a short-haul nature, continued in a long, drawn-out diminuendo. Symbolically, it was not until the motorways threw their concrete ribbons across the region that indigenous canal carriers like Thomas Clayton, T.S. Element and Alfred Matty began to give up their collective ghosts.

And what ghosts they left behind. For two decades the BCN lay moribund, a third of it abandoned beyond economic or socially desirable hope. It became valued, more than anything, domestically and industrially, as a linear rubbish dump. Though technically and legally open to navigation, all but the most tenacious boaters were deterred from entering the BCN by auguries of impassibility and hooliganism. The network needed soothsayers and visionaries

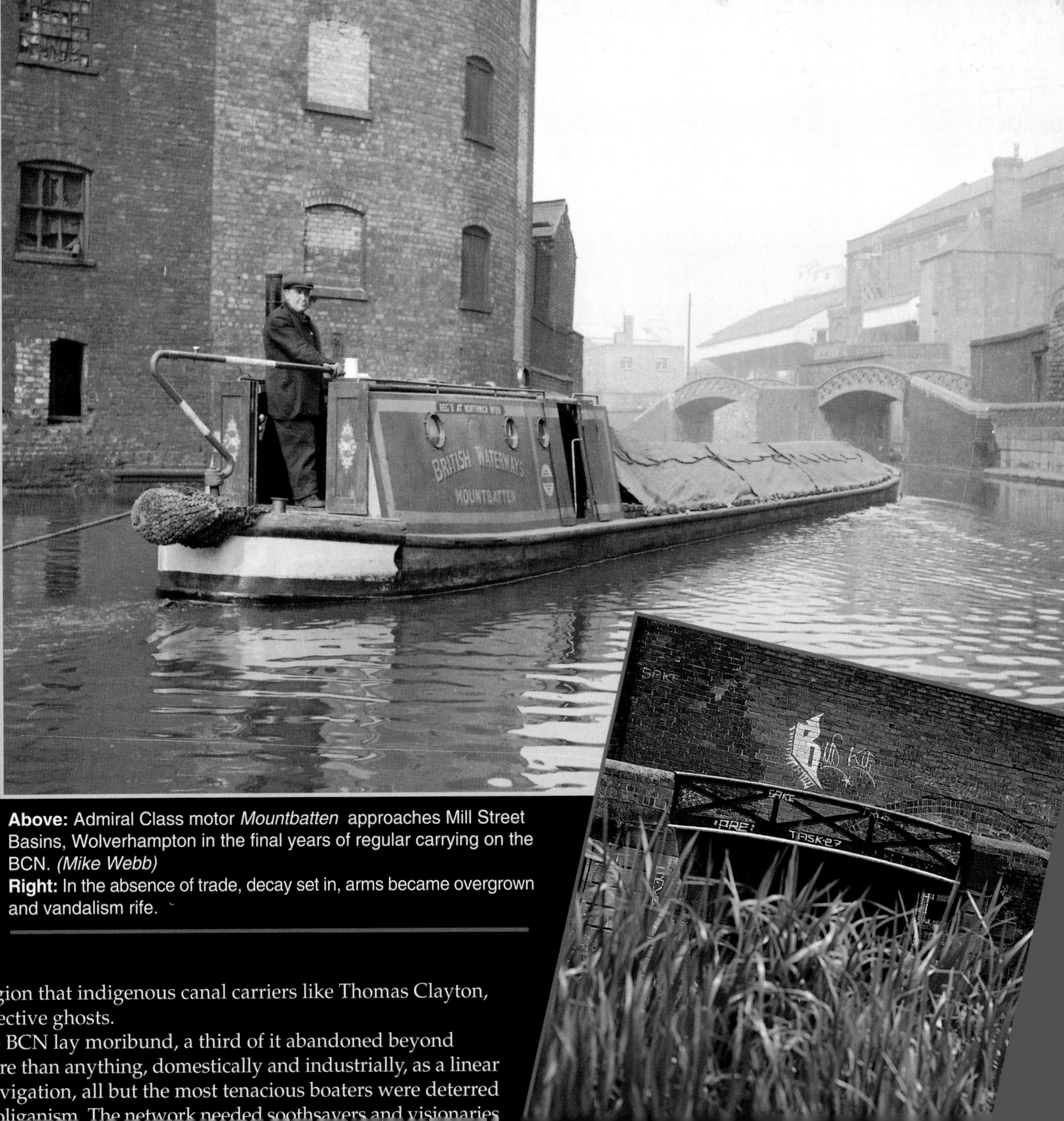

Above: Admiral Class motor *Mountbatten* approaches Mill Street Basins, Wolverhampton in the final years of regular carrying on the BCN. *(Mike Webb)*
Right: In the absence of trade, decay set in, arms became overgrown and vandalism rife.

if it was going to escape, recognisably inta
by the skin of its teeth.

Cometh the hour, cometh the canal fa
They came collectively in the shape of th
Birmingham Canal Navigations Society a
the Inland Waterways Association who
began to campaign, voluably, in the late
Sixties, for retention of the network. The
had few sympathisers at first, these
reactionaries with a weird, and suspicious
risible and possibly perverted interest in
filthy waterways, but gradually their
mysterious enthusiasm infected people i
high places, professional canal managers
councillors and developers who began t
see the potential for regeneration inhere
in the area's canals. After all, they had mo
of them than Venice, didn't they?

So somewhere on the wate
road from Dudley Port to
Damascus there was an offic
volte-face, a parody of *Anima
Farm* where suddenly the powe
that be were relaying the mantr
"Canals are Good - Roads are
Bad!"

They didn't mean that in a
cargo carrying sense, of course,
no-one would seriously suggest
that carrying by narrowboat
could be viable at the end of the
twentieth century, to do so woul
be heresy. No, in future the
BCN's role would be regenerative:
'new life for old canals!' So suddenly, instea
of demolishing canalside warehouses an
the associated architecture of the industri
revolution, the planners and developers

Main Picture: A fish-eye view of Thomas Telf
magnificent Galton Bridge, Smethwick, built in 1
Left inset: Galton Bridge with its eponymousl
named railway station to the rear.
Right inset: Contemporary mezzotint of Galto
Bridge, the width of the canal being somewhat
exaggerated by the artist.

pegan to utilise them - often quite imaginatively ınd successfully - as a means of regenerating areas of the West Midlands which had decayed almost ıs alarmingly as the canals themselves. British Naterways and the Birmingham City Council, with he aid of European funding, formed a 'Canal Partnership' to breath new life into run-down owpaths. Public access, which in the working ıeyday of the canal had been limited, was improved ınd increased, and the general public responded oositively by using the towpaths, recreationally, in heir thousands. Where boat horses once strained o pull twenty-five ton narrowboats, office workers sat on freshly provided benches to eat their lunch, or donned skimpy nylon running shorts and vests or jogging sessions which might take them as far rom the banks and boardrooms of Livery Street as Winson Green or Selly Oak or Aston.

From modest refurbishments, such as the Cincinatti factory frontage of the Birmingham & Fazeley Canal, massive schemes ensued. Gas Street Basin, to many the epitome of Birmingham's canal culture, and scene of the controversial demolition n 1975 of some historic, listed warehouses, was progressively redeveloped towards the end of the Eighties with new buildings, not a little ironically unlike those they'd replaced. Here, the only nterloper unsympathetic to the nineteenth century scale of the original, was the Hyatt Hotel, which ooked as though its blueprint had somehow got mixed up on the drawing board with one for a new hotel in Houston.

On the Dudley No.1 Canal the site of Round Oak Steelworks was transformed by the Richardson Brothers into the Merry Hill Centre, a complex of shopping malls and associated commercial and eisure developments.

But perhaps the most startling and ambitious use of the canals for regeneration was in the centre of Birmingham itself where the International

Gas Street Basin. The bricked-up archway at the end of the basin once led to the original, Suffolk Street terminus of the Birmingham Canal.

the Worcester Bar and Old Turn Junction. This was a
ransformation scene to be proud of. No other city in the country has succeeded so well in revitalising its legacy of industrial waterways. Manchester has its Castlefield, Leeds its Granary Wharf, London has nothing in the same league. Birmingham beats them all.

Winning, though, is one thing, but where do we go from here? Restoration must be followed by upkeep and maintenance if it isn't to be followed by regression. Plenty of modest refurbishment programmes around Birmingham and the Black Country have suffered from vandalism and neglect. The civil engineers wave their magic wands. There are photo opportunities and sound bites for the local media. Then the show moves to another worthy site. Meanwhile the graffiti artists emerge from the undergrowth, saplings sprout through the neatly laid gravel, puddles disfigure the resurfaced towpath and we are back to square one. Today's modest and laudable improvement becomes tomorrow's eyesore.

There are no easy answers other than a cast iron commitment to maintenance in the broadest sense. We should be on guard, too, against over-development. The canal infrastructure has to be allowed to keep its integrity within the context of new developments on its banks. It seems to manage this in central Birmingham but fails between Great Bridge and Darlaston where the Walsall Canal has been totally emasculated, suffocated and sterilized by the emergence of new business parks and housing zones along its banks. Only the most reactionary industrial archaeologist would argue that nothing should have been done to it, that it should have been left to decay romantically as a post industrial ruin, but it should have been treated with more respect, or rather, more imagination.

Entering a new millennium we must be positive and optimistic. British Waterways, guardians in many ways of our canals' destiny, are, thankfully, acutely aware of the significance of their heritage and have every intention of blending it appropriately and tactfully with redevelopment, as and when it occurs.

For years a traditional aspect of these canals was their use for the collection and carriage of refuse as characterised by the quaint, plodding passing of a canal horse and a day boat. Scenes like this could return, fulfilling several worthwhile functions at once. There are canalside incinerators at Wolverhampton and Tyseley. Collection depots could once again be sited on canal banks throughout the region and refuse boated to the incinerating plants. Road traffic would be reduced, the environment would be enhanced, and the canal could once again be used, modestly - and not a little picturesquely - for what it was built for.

The sermon's over. Let this modest introduction to the canals of Birmingham & the Black Country light fuses of enthusiasm. Get yourselves out there, on foot, by bike, afloat, and let the BCN start to weave its unique magic. Have fun!

Regeneration! The toll house at Winson Green has vanished, and so have the working boats, nowadays Birmingham's canals are enjoying new uses, as exemplified here by the coffee boat at Water's Edge.

Light & Shade

Main picture: Bean's Foundry, Tipton.
Upper left: Bow-hauling down 'The 21', Wolverhampton.
Lower left: Under the M5, Old Main Line near Smethwick.
Right: Canal busting on the Ridgacre Branch.

GRAND UNION APPROACHES

IN working boat days a steady stream of narrow boats - usually worked in pairs - traded up from London docks with all manner of cargo for the west midlands. This walk accompanies the Grand Union Canal - now a major long distance footpath in its own right - on its way into Birmingham past the sites and, in many cases, fascinating remnants, of a number of once important wharves and warehouses and, by using your imagination, you can rediscover much of the atmosphere of Birmingham's canal system in its commercial heyday.

Turn left outside Tyseley's attractively tiled booking hall (still furnished with authentic Great Western seating) and follow Kings Road down to the Grand Union Canal. It's a five minute walk made interesting by the survival of much 1930s industrial and commercial architecture, pinpointing the era in which these suburbs of Birmingham were developed.

The Grand Union Canal itself dates from the Thirties too, by virtue of being an amalgamation of a series of individual canals linking London with Birmingham. The route you will follow into Birmingham was opened as the Warwick & Birmingham Canal in 1799. It was incorporated into the Grand Union in 1929 and the wharves at Tyseley and Sampson Road date from a subsequent period of expansion and modernisation. Tyseley Wharf was equipped to deal with heavy cargoes such as steel.

Join the towpath, pass beneath Bridge 88 and head for the city centre. Note the winding hole now covered with lily pads where boats would turn back for London after unloading. An imposing concrete side bridge carries the towpath over what was once a busy arm taking boats in and out of a dock serving the Hay Mills Incinerator. Horse-drawn boats were still bringing Birmingham's refuse here as recently as 1965.

Further echoes of industrial activity accompany the canal on its way through Small Heath and Bordesley. Either side of the former Great Western Railway's crossing of the canal, side bridges span the site of arms which once led into the famous Birmingham Small Arms factory. One of the former boat docks has been adapted for use by the Ackers Trust for youth related water activities. By Bridge 90 look out for a former refuse basin overlooked by a distinctively clock-towered pub. Sampson Road and Bordesley Goods Depot are two forgotten points where water and rail borne consignments were discharged or loaded, delivered or stored in previous eras of transport. Now, of course, the bulk of Birmingham's freight arrives or leaves by road and both the canal and railway depot are simply used for storage, though there is an ironic use of the railway sidings for the carriage of cars by rail.

Camp Hill derives its name from doings in the neighbourhood during the Civil War. These days boaters battle their way up and down a flight of six locks couched in a thoroughly urban landscape dominated by the deconsecrated Georgian Gothic of Holy Trinity church. The third lock down was re-sited to make way for a road widening. When the Grand Union Canal was modernised in the 1930s, widening of these locks was considered, but rejected on the grounds that most cargoes would be finishing their journeys by road in any case, and that they might just as well be discharged at Tyseley or Sampson Road rather than continue into the heart of the city by water.

Factories start hemming you in towards the bottom of the Camp Hill flight: engaged in inscrutable activities accompanied by humming, grinding and hammering, you can only guess at the nature of each business. Immediately beyond the the bottom lock a handsome, cast iron roving bridge carries the towpath over the Grand Union's 'Saltley Cut' which threads its way through '"Heartlands" to meet the Birmingham & Fazeley Canal at Salford Junction, an ancient meeting place of canals all but submerged by the concrete conundrum of Spaghetti Junction. In boating terms this route is popular with holidaymakers doing "The Warwickshire Ring" who skirt Birmingham, oblivious to the BCN's inherent charm.

Overlooked by Birmingham Central Garage, a huge bus depot, the Grand Union proceeds towards its terminus at Warwick Bar. Naturally you can stay on the towpath if you prefer, but a short detour through adjoining streets is to be recommended. Join Great Barr Street at Bridge 95. Cross the canal and turn right into Fazeley Street. The male of the species can still take advantage of the cast iron urinal on the corner of the street, one of a handful of survivors from a once ubiquitous feature of the city's commercial districts.

Fazeley Street is almost quite literally endlessly fascinating and full of buildings with tales to tell. "The Bond" is a complex of art studios housed in buildings once used by an ice manufacturing company and canalside warehouses formerly belonging to Fellows Morton & Clayton. Their basin is still in water and occasionally used for moorings by passing boaters. Spurred on by modernisation of the Grand Union - even if the locks weren't widened this far! - FMC opened a new warehouse on Fazeley Street in 1935. Their name is still emblazoned on the street side facade, engendering a very real sense of canal history; so much so, that you half expect working narrow boats to be congregated on the cut at the rear, where the wall is stylishly curved with maritime overtones.

Rejoin the towpath where Fazeley Street crosses the entrance to basins at the end of the Birmingham & Fazeley's Digbeth Branch. This is the scene depicted on this book's front cover. Behind a high brick wall the Gun Barrel Proof House has been the scene of weapons testing since 1813. Directly opposite a roving bridge carries the towpath over

Opposite page: Ox eye daises carpet the canal bank at Camp Hill Top lock with the former Sampson Road canal depot behind.

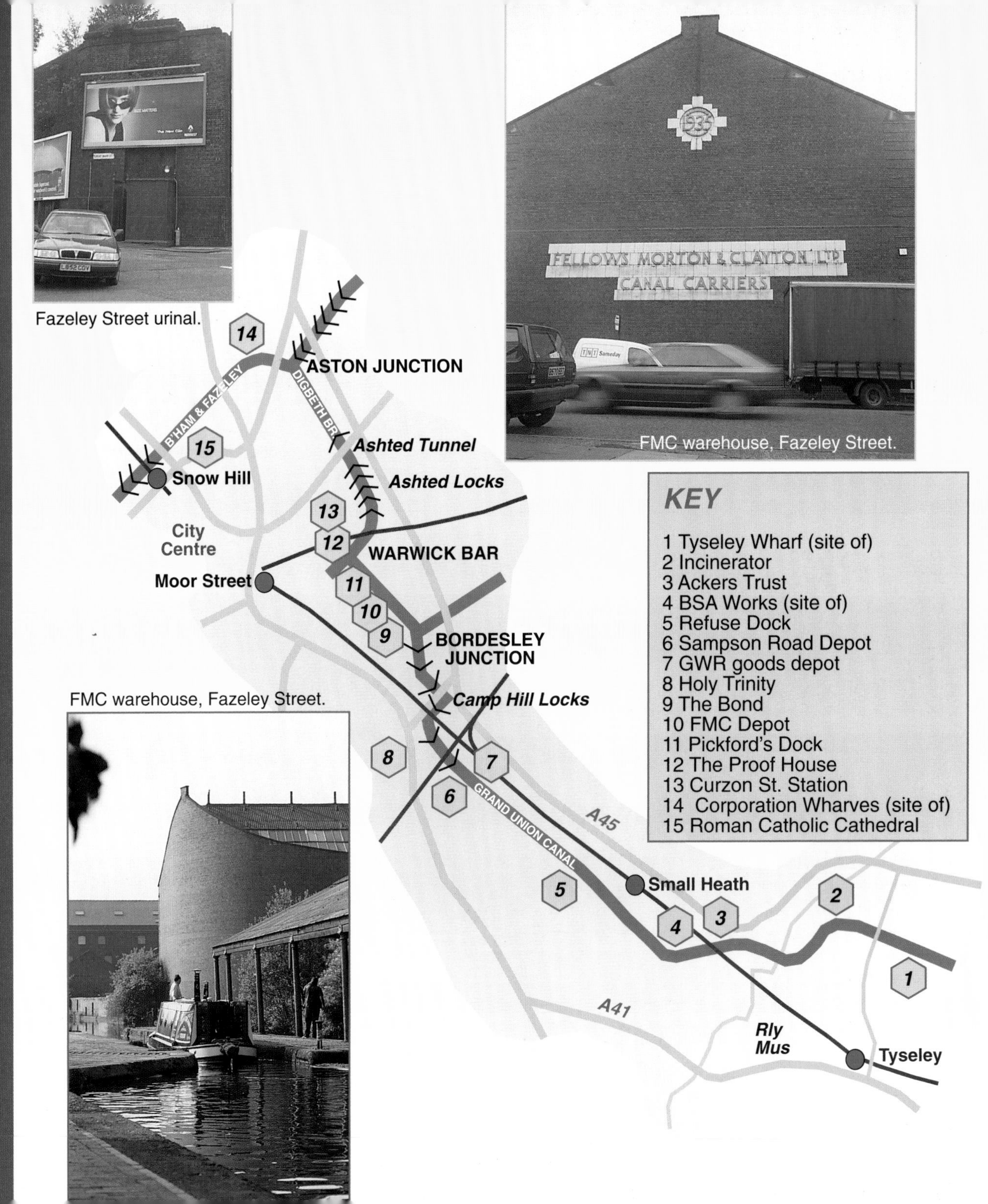

Fazeley Street urinal.

FMC warehouse, Fazeley Street.

FMC warehouse, Fazeley Street.

the entrance to the Grand Union Canal and Warwick Bar, the site of a stop lock which once jealously guarded the individual canal company's water supplies. Spare a moment to peep under the adjoining bridge and admire the covered dock (pictured on the previous page) which once belonged to Pickfords, and rummage in the undergrowth to find the base of Warwick Bar's former toll office. Look too, southwards towards Bordesley, where the canal is carried over the River Rea and where the towpath surges upwards to cross what was once an arm serving yet another refuse depot. Then spend a moment envisaging the activity here when canal transport was at its zenith.

The Digbeth Branch is being regenerated with a bang - Millennium Point will be close by. A long, curving tunnel takes the canal beneath the busy railway lines of Proof House Junction and the approaches to New Street station. Look back at the attractive northern portal which dates back to the arrival of the Grand Junction Railway at the imposingly Ionic Curzon Street station, which it shared with the London & Birmingham Railway, in 1838. The old station, ignored by passengers since the opening of the more centrally located New Street in 1854, still commands the neighbourhood and is well worth a detour along Curzon Street at this point.

The six Ashted Locks carry the Digbeth Branch from 336 feet above sea level at Warwick Bar to 372 feet at Aston Junction. They are characterful chambers with sizeable side ponds and single gates top and tail as per BCN practice. Halfway up the flight a curious little BCN employee's house (numbered 65 in the BCN sequence) overlooks the canal, an oasis of domesticity in a desert of industrial activity.

Ashted Tunnel has a towpath and is lighted for the benefit of the increasing numbers of pedestrians, joggers and cyclists who've discovered the calming influence of these secretive routes in the city. It's only just over a hundred yards long, but it effects a stunning scene change as the canal emerges from a largely 19th century environment into the Brave New World of Aston Science Park. Surrounded by high tech activities, the canal continues to Aston Junction like a strand of 18th century fibre somehow woven into a 21st century garment. A series of chronologically challenged brick overbridges span the canal's progress to the junction. The new industries benefit from the canal cosmetically, but old side bridges indicate that there was once trade here too.

Left: Holy Trinity Church dominates the Camp Hill flight as a traditionally styled BCN tug enters the fourth lock up, where the old Great Western line into Snow Hill crosses the canal.

A Horseley Iron Works cast iron roving bridge creates piquant contrast with the concrete civil engineering of the adjacent Expressway at Aston Junction. Hurtling into the city centre, few motorists have any conception of the fragile 18th century world below them. But you have time to assimilate the gulf in architectural styles. When you've finished, bear left towards Birmingham, passing beneath the Expressway and following the towpath of the Birmingham & Fazeley Canal back to Snow Hill.

A series of switchback side bridges carries the towpath over what was once a trio of arms serving Birmingham Corporation wharves. Ahead of you the BT telecommunications tower begins to dominate the horizon. Barker Bridge is perhaps the most significant feature of this length of canal. Dating from 1842 it features, on one side at least, a graceful cast iron span supported by brick piers and abutments. And if you've been wondering what all these little red doors on bridge parapets are, the explanation is that they're there for the benefit of firefighters, who can thrust their hoses through them and extract canal water until any flames in the locality are well and truly doused.

As your walk nears its close, there's a glimpse of the twin spires of Birmingham's Roman Catholic Cathedral, St Chads, followed by the sobering sight of the Salvation Army hostel, oddly juxtaposed with an area of upwardly mobile financial businesses. Leave the canal at Snow Hill Bridge and go up Constitution Hill and over St Chads Circus to return to Snow Hill railway station.

Information

OS reference: SP110840 **AZ** 2G 91

Access: Frequent trains connect Tyseley station with Birmingham Moor Street and Snow Hill.

Refreshments: There are cafes on Kings Road where you'll find enough calories to set you on your way. In Digbeth, Fazeley Street features "The Forge Tavern", a cafe at "The Bond" and a cafe adjacent to the basins at the end of the Digbeth Branch.

Right: BCN house by Belmont Row Bridge on the Ashted flight. Just one more lap to go!

LOOPING THE LOOPS

BRINDLEY'S canal from Birmingham to Wednesbury, opened in 1769, went out of its way to avoid every small protusion in its path, more than doubling the distance rather than incur complicated and expensive earthworks. Telford's improvements, on the other hand, completed seventy years later, run absolutely straight all the way from Ladywood to Winson Green. Through traffic, naturally, took to Telford's new route like juggernauts to a new motorway, but Brindley's old loops remained very much in use to serve already well established works and wharves along their winding banks. Most of these loops remain navigable to this day, retained, in latter years, not so much as a consequence of trade, but for the part they play in drainage and water supply. The New Main Line sliced off five loops between Birmingham and Smethwick: the Oozells Street, Icknield Port and Soho loops remain and are often included in the itineraries of trip boats operating from Gas Street and the International Convention Centre. So, on this occasion, there's no excuse for not taking to the water to explore these particular environs of the BCN, especially as, in any case, the Oozells Street and Icknield Port loops are towpathless.

Each of the old loops has its own atmosphere and character. The Oozells Street Loop begins almost on the steps of the ICC at Old Turn Junction, its egress from the main line being overlooked by the Indoor Arena and Sea Life Centre. It curves away past new blocks of smart flats to Sherborne Street Wharf, once an important canal carrying depot, but now a busy boatyard of the leisure age. Completing its arc, the Oozells Street Loop rejoins the main line beneath the modern equivalent of a BCN roving bridge, look, opposite, for the old Corporation 'horseshoe' stable block, part of which is now converted into a pub.

The next loop to tempt explorers away from Telford's route is at Icknield Port. Having passed the old railway interchange basin

Monument Lane, and gone beneath Birmingham's inner ring road, the main line runs parallel with the railway and the loop disappears off in a southerly direction between high factory walls. A large embankment holds the canal supply waters of Rotton Park Reservoir in place as the loop passes the site of a former British Waterways maintenance yard notable for its handsome Telford designed office.

Rotton Park Junction forms a canal crossroads as, crossing the main line, the Icknield Port Loop becomes the Soho Loop and heads for Winson Green via Hockley Port. At Hockley Port there was a busy transhipment depot operated by the Great Western Railway. Nowadays it's a thriving centre for residential moorings.

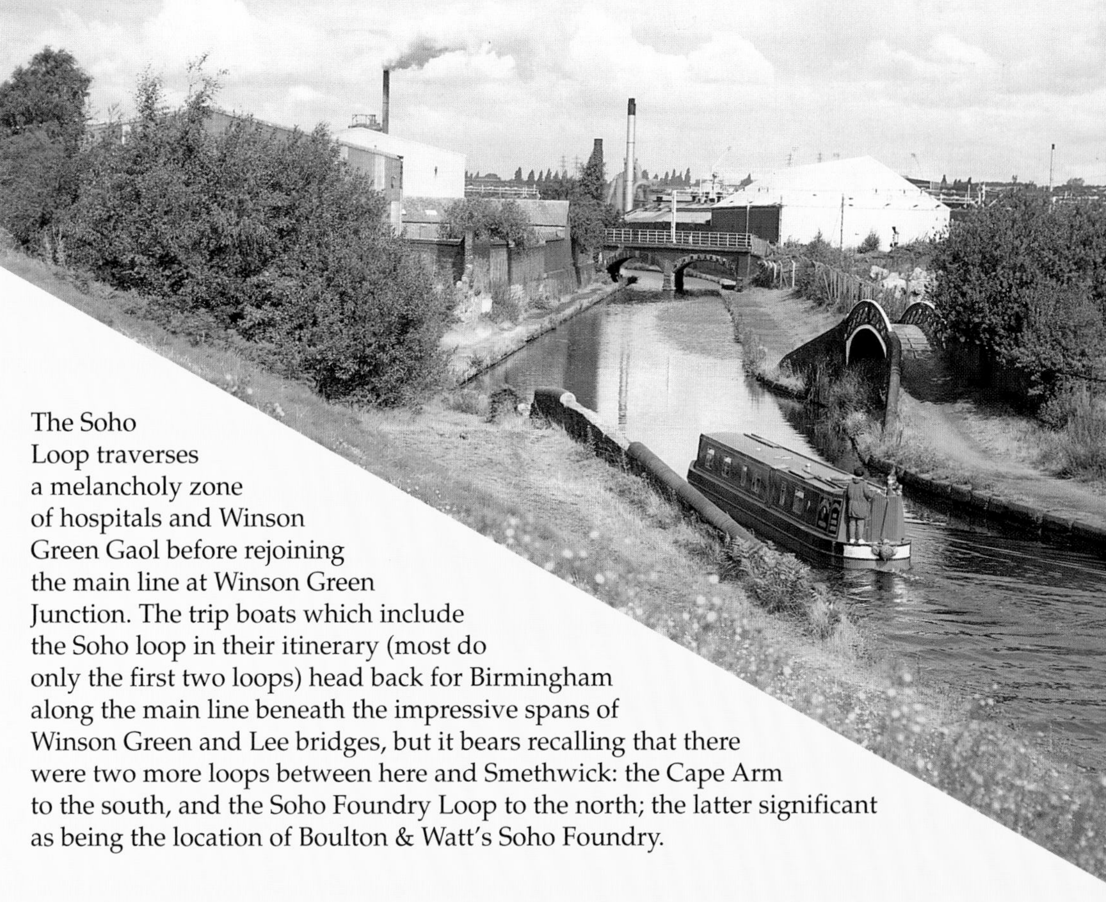

The Soho Loop traverses a melancholy zone of hospitals and Winson Green Gaol before rejoining the main line at Winson Green Junction. The trip boats which include the Soho loop in their itinerary (most do only the first two loops) head back for Birmingham along the main line beneath the impressive spans of Winson Green and Lee bridges, but it bears recalling that there were two more loops between here and Smethwick: the Cape Arm to the south, and the Soho Foundry Loop to the north; the latter significant as being the location of Boulton & Watt's Soho Foundry.

Information

OS reference: SP062866 **AZ** 3A 152

The following companies operate regular trip boat services from the International Convention Centre, Gas Street or Brindley Place.

Sherborne Wharf - 0121 455 6163.

Parties Afloat - 0121 236 7057.

Captions

Title picture: *Euphrates* emerges on to the Main Line at Rotton Park Junction.
Opposite lower: Winson Green Junction.
This page left: *Jericho* at Monument Lane.
This page above: The Cape Arm.

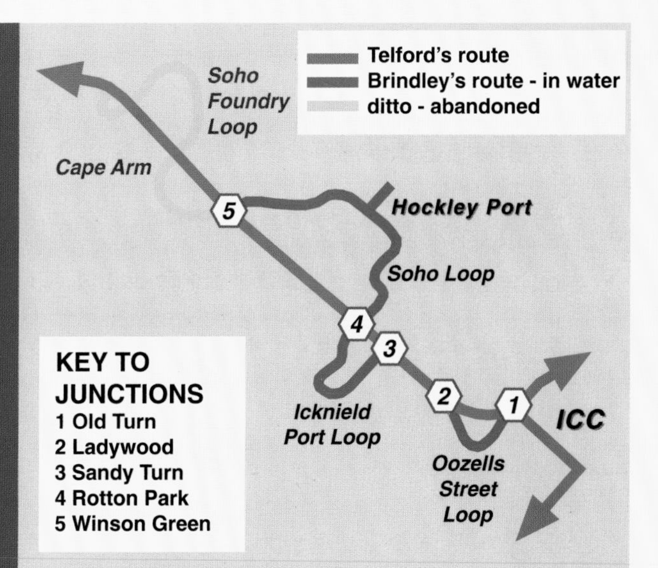

SMETHWICK

SMETHWICK boasts one of the great canalscapes in the country. Climb the footbridge, which offers pedestrians a short cut between Brasshouse Lane and Smethwick town centre, and you're presented with a panoramic view of the two main lines coming in from Wolverhampton past the imposing redbrick Pumping House of 1892 and proceeding towards Birmingham in sweeping curves. From this superb vantage point you can also trace the line of Brindley's original route, a short summit running along the 491ft contour. This was approached through six locks at either end. Less than a mile long, it was bedevilled by operating difficulties. In 1790, John Smeaton, best known for his work on the Eddystone Rock lighthouse, lowered the summit by eighteen feet to its present position. He built three new locks at the Smethwick Junction end, though Brindley's corresponding bottom three were retained as duplicates until as recently as 1960. Ferret about in the undergrowth and you can still find evidence of their existence. Much of the delight to be gained for canal exploration lies in the peeling back of layers of time.

Leave your eyrie and follow Brasshouse Lane to the Canal Heritage Centre (Tel: 0121-558 8195 to check opening hours), a useful port of call at which to stock up on local leaflets and learn, from the fascinating exhibits on display, more of the background to the history of Smethwick's canals than we have space to devote to here. Not so long ago this was a public house called the Cock Inn. Much longer ago a boatman's pub called the White Swan stood, along with some canal employees cottages, at the foot of the ramp which runs down to the canals from Brasshouse Lane.

Brasshouse Lane derives its name from a foundry which stood to the north of the Old Main Line. By the middle of the 19th century the market for brass had declined and the works went over to iron and steel. It was still in business early in the 1990s. During tea breaks, workers, many of them turbaned Sikhs, would come and cool off on the wall overlooking the canal. They're gone now, and so is their foundry, the site having been razed and left as wasteground pending redevelopment.

A typical humpbacked canal bridge carries the towpath over the entrance to the Engine Arm, a short, dogleg shaped arm constructed primarily as a feeder from Rotton Park Reservoir, but also to enable boats to carry coal to the original pumping engine on Bridge Street. Any boat lengthier than thirty feet which chooses to explore it now has to back out the way it came, for there is no turning point at the far end. But enthusiastic boaters do take the trouble to explore this forgotten branch, largely for the thrill of crossing Telford's astonishingly elegant iron aqueduct which was cast at the Horseley Iron Works in Tipton. Just look at that exquisite Gothic detail in the ironwork, and marvel that such care should be extended towards such an irrelevant backwater. Mind you, of course, the aqueduct does

"unsurpassed in stupendous magnificence". We'll bring you back this way, meanwhile follow the locks down to Smethwick Junction, spanned like its counterpart at Bromford, by two Horseley roving bridges. Turn back along the New Main Line and follow it through its cutting as far as the aqueduct, noting the site of the gauging station on the way. Tolls were calculated here by measuring each boat's height out of the water, and thus the amount of cargo it was carrying..

Ascend to the upper level and cross the aqueduct, continuing along the Engine Arm towpath as far as Bridge Street. Join the road here and make your way up to the junction with Rolfe Street. This was the site of the original Smethwick Pumping Engine. Built in 1779 by James Watt, it was designed to pump water up the six locks to Brindley's summit. It worked successfully for a century until the new pumping engine on Brasshouse Lane was commissioned. Such was its age and significance, that Henry Ford tried to buy it and have it shipped to America. Fortunately he failed and for many years it took pride of place in Birmingham's Museum of Science & Industry. Hopefully it will re-emerge at Millennium Point in due course.

Opposite page: Smethwick Junction. (Title picture shows junction post at entrance to Engine Arm).
Below: The Engine Arm viewed from the level of Brindley's original summit section.
Inset: Map consulting cyclists.
Right above: Gothic detail from the Engine Arm Aqueduct.

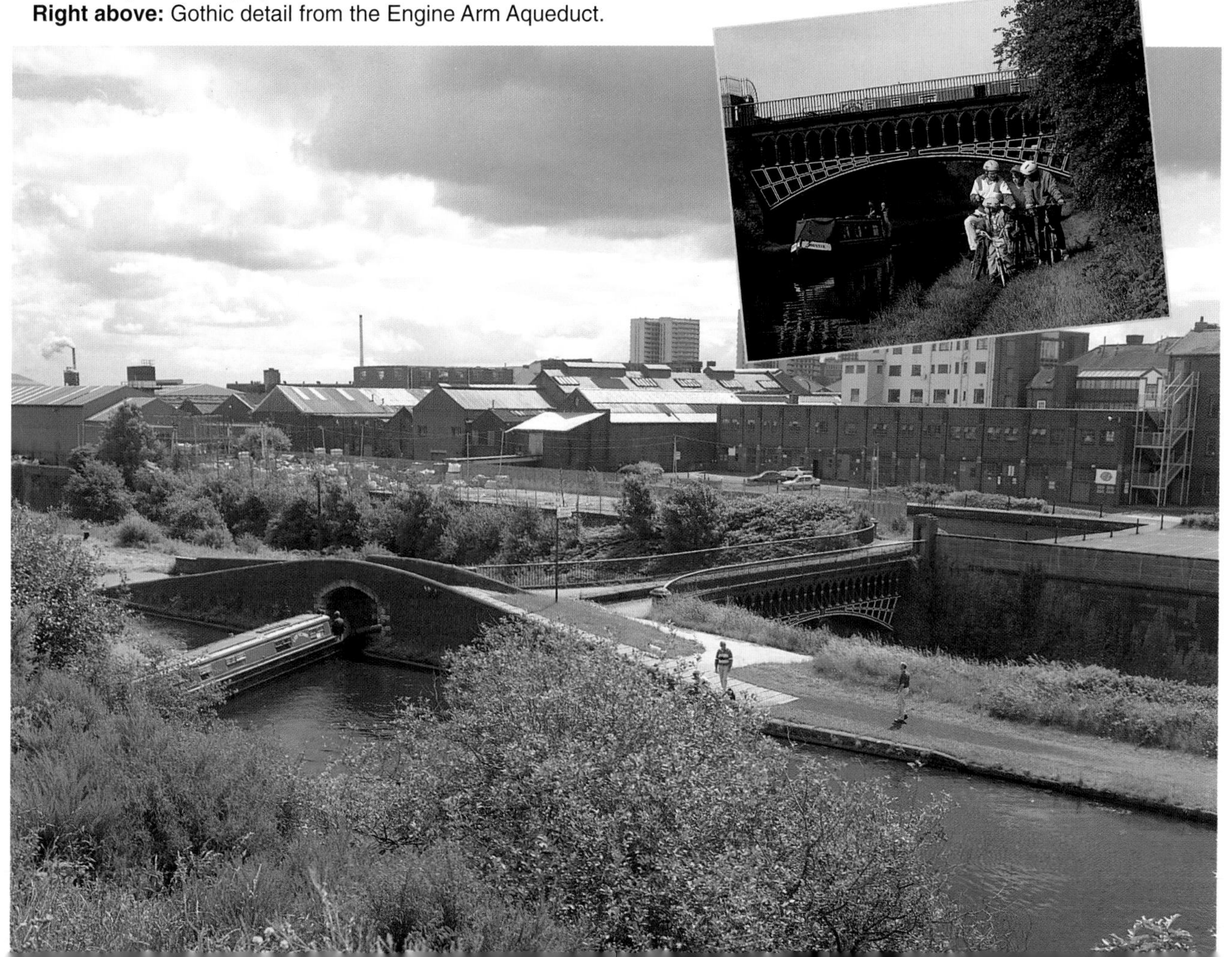

Information

OS reference: SP020890 **AZ** 1A 72

Access: Frequent trains connect Smethwick Rolfe Street station with Birmingham New Street, International, Coventry and Wolverhampton. Public access to the canal and car parking is provided at Galton Valley Canal Heritage Centre on Brasshouse Lane just off the A457.

Refreshments: Plenty of shops in Smethwick (many of them of Asian persuasion if you've a weakness for bhajees - as opposed to bargees!) but few salubrious pubs worth recommending.

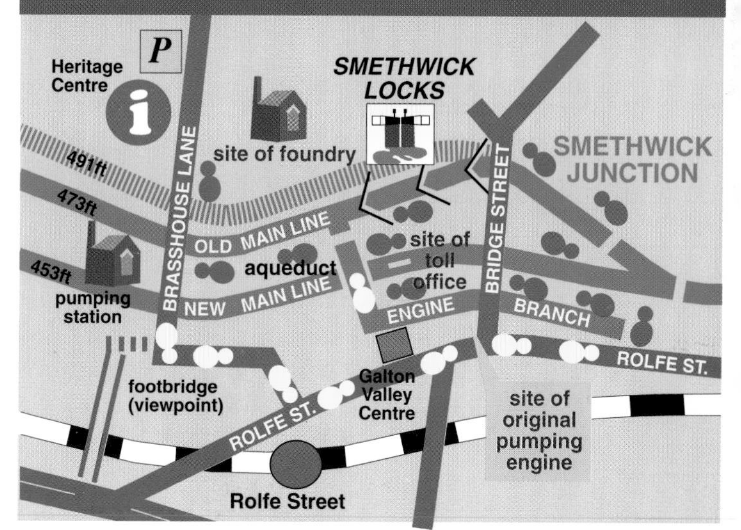

The TITFORD Canal

DEEP in the malodorous, chemical making landscape of Langley, on the south-eastern outskirts of Oldbury, lies the Titford Canal, a mile and a half long branch off the Old Main Line which climbs through six locks to the Birmingham Canal Navigation's loftiest summit pound, 511 feet above sea level. Even by BCN standards it's a backwater, rarely boated except for

Kevin Maslin

campaigning cruises and the occasional rally in Titford Pools, its southern terminus. So the of encountering a boat on the move are limited unless you've taken the trouble to bring your own. But there are ghosts of boats a plenty, for, right up until the mid 1960s, this was a busy canal, as you will see on your travels.

In the absence of a boat, turn right out of Langley Green's neat new clock-towered station, and follow Western Road to its confluence with Tat Bank Road. Chemical smells assault your nostrils, and there's a satisfying sense of being in the heart of a busy industrial setting. Go left along Tat Bank Road, past the imposing portals of British Industrial Plastics who use the Tat Bank Branch as a source of cooling water. Peep over the parapet of the branch to satisfy your curiosity. Once this was navigable, now its merely used as a water supply channel. Tat Bank Road crosses the Titford Canal itself, but you should ignore any temptation to join the towpath at this point, proceeding instead beneath the M5 motorway and joining the Old Main Line at Stone Street Bridge. Between here and Oldbury Locks Junction stood the boatyard of Thomas Clayton, specialists in the carriage of bulk liquids. Their fleet of eighty boats, distinguished by their flat decked holds, and named after rivers, was a significant facet of Black Country boating. Here is how Pearson's Canal Companion to the Stourport Ring (which modesty forbids we praise too highly) describes their operation. "Clayton's best known long distance traffic was the carriage of oil from Ellesmere Port to Shell's depot at Langley Green, a contract which lasted from 1924 to

Information

OS reference: SP996885 **AZ** 1E 71

Access: Half-hourly trains connect Langley Green station with Birmingham Snow Hill and there are connections at Galton Bridge with the New Street - Wolverhampton line.

Refreshments: The "Finings & Firkin" stands alongside Station Road Bridge and brews on the premises as it did in its previous existence as HPD's "Brewery Inn". Children and pets are frowned upon but that can only be a bonus to you "solitary, middle-aged men".

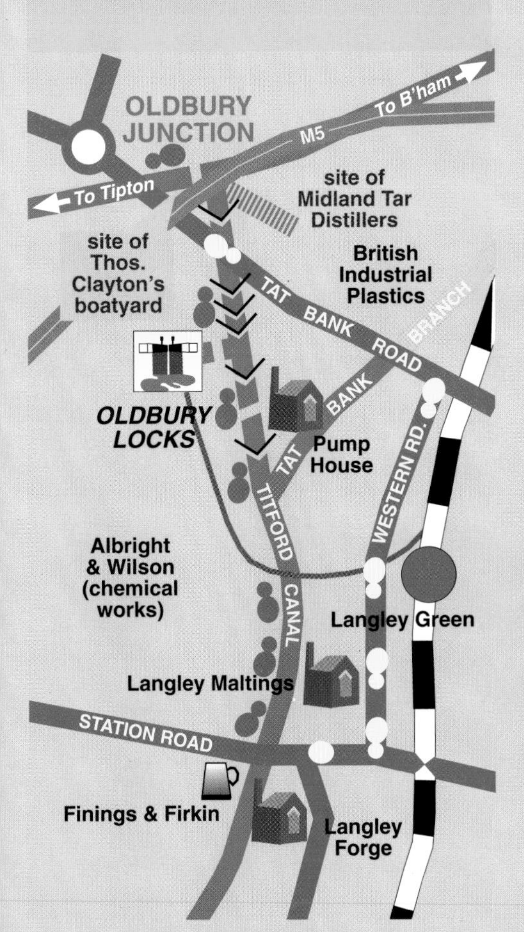

until 1955, some of the boats remaining horse-drawn until virtually the end. Clayton boats served the gasworks at Oxford, Banbury, Leamington and Solihull, but the bulk of their trade was of a more localised nature, notably the carriage of gas bi-products such as tar. Their last cargo - carried aboard the now preserved motor *Stour* - arrived at Midland Tar Distillers from Walsall Gasworks on 31st March 1966. Faced with diminishing cargoes (brought about largely by the advent of North Sea gas) and the disruption caused by construction of the M5, Thomas Clayton called it a day as far as canal transport was concerned." Little trace remains of the boatyard now. Disappeared also is the once vast tar distillery which marked the entrance to the Titford Canal.

Cross the concrete roving bridge and follow the towpath up Oldbury Locks. The lock-keeper's single-storey house is still used residentially, though now a firm timber fence separates it from inquisitive passers-by on the canal. Above Lock No.4 the towpath is carried across an arm which was used until the mid-Sixties by boats carrying phosphorous waste from the Albright & Wilson's chemical works. Back in those days the Titford Canal was riddled with chemical waste from the adjoining plants. Cyanide was a particular ingredient of this noxious recipe. The retrenchment of heavy industry and the tightening of waste disposal regulations has done much to make the Titford water considerably cleaner.

A semi-derelict, blue brick pumping house overlooks the top lock and the egress of the erstwhile Tat Bank Branch already encountered on your travels. Then the canal is crossed by what was once the Great Western Railway's Oldbury Branch, closed to passengers as long ago as the Great War, but used until quite recently for the shunting of chemical wagons in and out of Albright & Wilson.

Langley Maltings date from the 1890s. These days they belong to the Wolverhampton & Dudley Brewery Company whose beers are brewed in the former town under the Banks's banner. Ironically the little pub on the bridge carrying Station Road across the canal belongs to a different brewing company altogether. Neither does Langley Forge function any more, its huge drop-hammer, which used to shake the earth beneath your feet if you stood inquisitively in the doorway when it was operating, perennially and sadly now silent. Go back to the station and be glad that something, at least, of the old atmosphere of the Titford Canal has survived in the face of dereliction and redevelopment.

Title picture: Tat Bank Pumphouse.
Top right opposite: Boating past Tat Bank.
This page: Langley Maltings.
Inset: Titford bollard, Lock 4.

BROMFORD BRIDGE & SPON LANE

YOU emerge from Sandwell & Dudley's modern, split-level railway station into a part of Oldbury given over almost entirely to Black Country metal-bashing . The rail-link minibus to Dudley leaves in a cloud of dust, abandoning you to the 'interior'; a last link, with what passes for civilisation in these benighted parts, severed. Two hundred yards northwards along Bromford Road stands Bromford Bridge and the New Main Line.

Bromford Junction lies a short walk, along the well-surfaced towpath, to the east. The base of a toll office remains islanded at the point where the canal bifurcates, and you can't help but regret that none of these neat octagonal toll offices, once so characteristic of the BCN, have survived at any of their former locations. Two handsome, cast iron roving bridges make up for this loss. One spans what was Brindley's original Wednesbury 'Old' Canal, which ascends beyond this point, via three locks to the Wolverhampton Level. These locks are quite possibly the oldest working chambers in the country, and as such are listed structures. They see all too little use these days, most boats passing through Bromford sticking doggedly to Telford's route. Once, though, they were the scene of one of the most intriguing occurrences in the history of the area's canals. Here, between 1861 and 1890 the evangelist John Skidmore held weekly, open air revivalist meetings each summer. Attendances peaked at an incredible twenty thousand souls. According to Skidmore's diaries the throngs would assemble on slag heaps bordering the middle lock. "Thousands worshipped God in the open air ... rich and poor, old and young, well-dressed and ragged, drapers, grocers, butchers, tailors, publicans, ironmasters, clerks, magistrates, puddlers, coalmasters, mine agents, collieres, navvies, boatmen, roadmen, labourers, sweeps, a goodly number of Frenchmen from the Glass House, the aged and infirm, the lame and the blind, men of all creeds and no creed at all." Skidmore had been inspired to hold the meetings when, whilst out distributing tracts, he'd come upon a gathering of colliers and ironworkers at Spon Lane engaged in cockfighting and dog-fighting, gambling and whippet-racing. Through sheer force of personality the then youthful missionary persuaded these rough diamonds to attend an evangelist meeting on the spot the following Sunday. The meetings continued for nearly thirty years until the canal company reclaimed the land.

Strolling up the flight now, you need all the imagination you can muster to visualize the *al fresco* congregation, moved, in turn, to laughter and tears by Skidmore's oratory. There must have been times when they made as much noise as the crowd at West Bromwich Albion's nearby Hawthorns ground. Nowadays the noise comes from the crunching of cars in the neighbouring scrapyard and the incessant roar of traffic from the elevated section of the M5 motorway. The top lock is all but engulfed by the road, its tiny, cantilevered, cast iron tail bridge provoking piquant contrast with the motorway's massive concrete pillars and girders.

The lock lifts you up to the Old Main Line which proceeds on its gloomy,

Captions

Opposite page: Bromford Junction looking east towards Birmingham, the elevated M5 motorway runs across the picture in the distance.
Above: Two generations of civil engineering on show as a narrow boat waits to enter Spon Lane Top Lock.
Left: Bizarre boating territory as a cabin cruiser passes a heap of scrapped car components on the Old Main Line at Spon Lane.

almost subterranean way under the gloom of the motorway towards Smethwick. Two significant Victorian industrial premises stand in varying degrees of decay on either side of Spon Lane Bridge. To the north (and a notable landmark to motorway travellers) is the Gothic, church-like clocktower of Archibald Kenrick's ironmongery foundry. To the south, on an island site between the old and new main lines, are the remains of Chance's glassworks. Glass for the Great Exhibition of 1851 was manufactured here, and in its heyday over a thousand employees were kept busy in the works which expanded to fill sites on either side of the New Main Line and the parallel 'Stour Valley' rail route linking Birmingham and Wolverhampton.

Retracing your steps from Spon Lane Bridge (by way of the south side towpath) you come upon the graceful and elegant Steward Aqueduct, built to Telford's designs in 1828 to carry the Old Main Line over his new route. It was named after a prominent BCN director of the period. Steps lead down to the lower level which you can follow back to Bromford Junction.

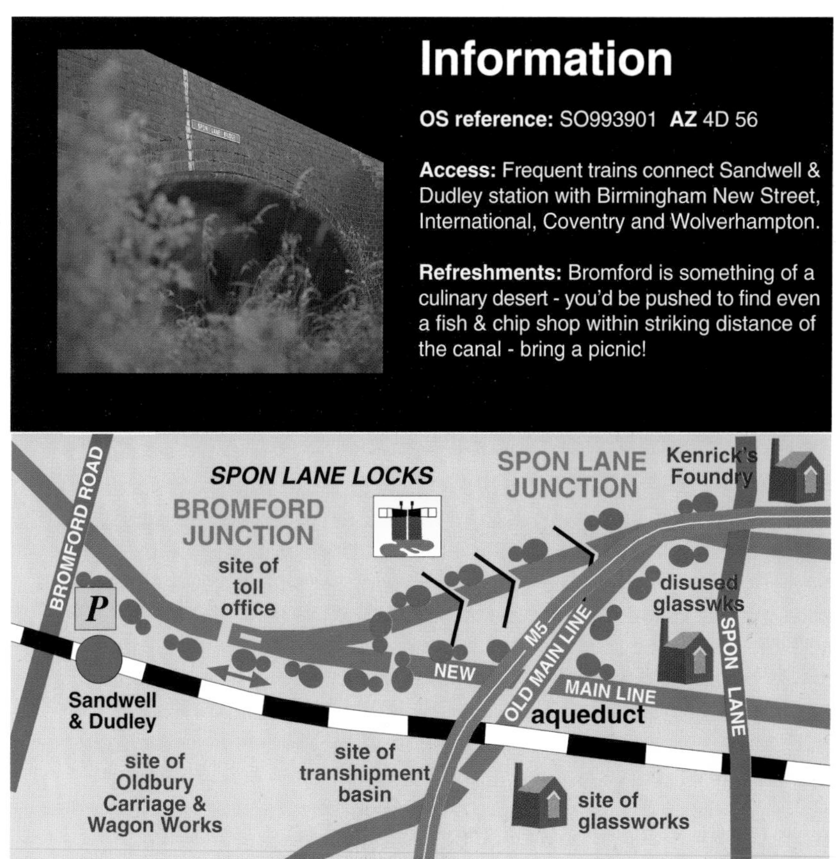

Information

OS reference: SO993901 **AZ** 4D 56

Access: Frequent trains connect Sandwell & Dudley station with Birmingham New Street, International, Coventry and Wolverhampton.

Refreshments: Bromford is something of a culinary desert - you'd be pushed to find even a fish & chip shop within striking distance of the canal - bring a picnic!

DUDLEY PORT & TIVIDALE

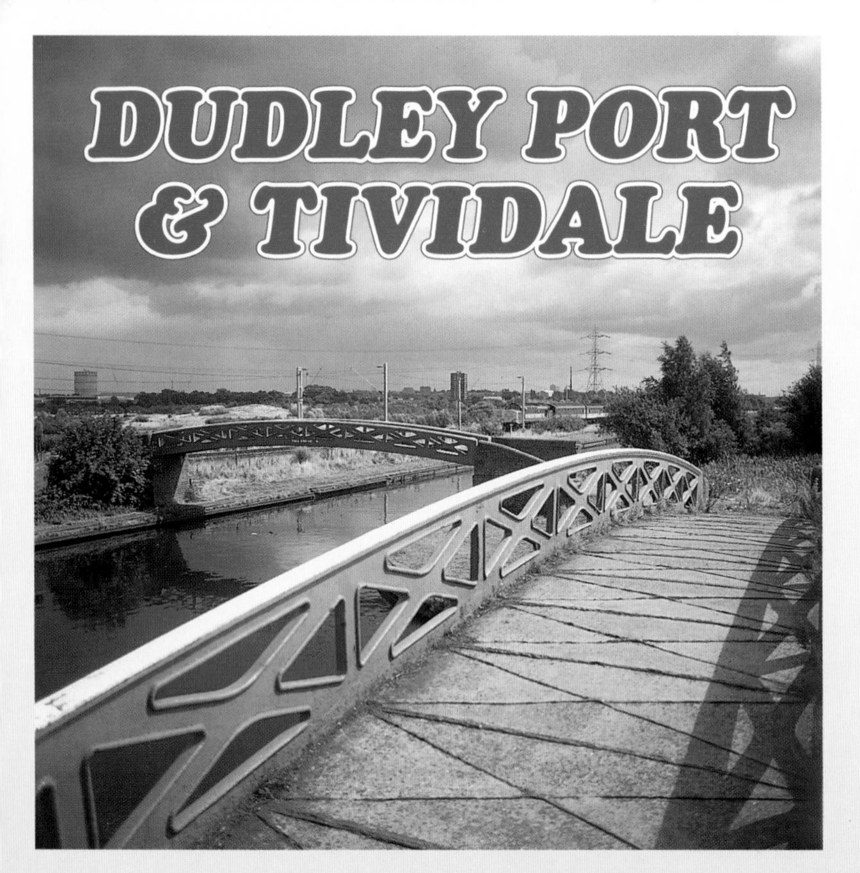

A short walk from Dudley Port railway station encompasses both Brindley's and Telford's main lines and two interesting branches. Turn right at the foot of the station incline and pass under the canal; the latter is carried across the road on an ornate, modern aqueduct dating from the widening of the A461 in 1968. Cross the road (carefully!) and go up the steps to join the towpath. Bear right along the New Main Line engineered in the 1820s by Thomas Telford, the equivalent of a modern day relief road.

At Dudley Port Junction the Netherton Branch heads south to pass beneath the Rowley Hills (by way of a long tunnel you'll see later on your walk) to join the Dudley Canal at Windmill End. A pair of 'Toll End Works' roving bridges (pictured above) create pleasing symmetries in this oddly remote spot. Bulrushes grow in the marshy remains of a basin which once served the Stour Valley New Brick Works.

Parallel with the busy railway, past wastegrounds once worked extensively for clay extraction, Telford's route proceeds to Albion Junction where the base of a former toll island remains intact, posing problems for nervous boat steerers. Once this was a watery crossroads but there's little indication on the ground of where the Dunkirk Branch, abandoned in 1953, once passed beneath the railway and headed a short distance northwards into a wasteland of gravel pits and abandoned coal shafts, in the vicinity of Greets Green. Note the sculptured, cast iron figure of a horse facing the railway one of a series erected in the late eighties as part of a 'greening' programme along the railway corridor between Birmingham and Wolverhampton.

Cross the roving bridge and turn right along the towpath of the Gower Branch. Comparatively rural in appearance, it climbs through three locks to link with Brindley's Old Main Line at Brades Hall Junction. The upper lock, spanned by the A457, is a 'staircase' lock, where the two chambers share a common centre gate. Such arrangements saved space but proved time consuming to use and caused delays. This is the only one on the whole of the BCN system.

Turn right across the girder roving bridge and follow the towpath to Tividale. It's immediately apparent how Brindley's canal differs in character from Telford's. Most obviously it meanders rather than running straight - the engineering techniques, and the confidence in them, of the 1770s weren't as sophisticated as those prevalent fifty years later. Brindley preferred to hug the contours, thus keeping earthworks to a minimum.

Build a new road these days and it's bound to attract industrial estates. In much the same way Brindley's Birmingham - Wolverhampton canal brought a rush of activity to its banks. The Ordnance Survey six inch map of 1904 indicates no less than seven arms stretching southwards off the main canal in the short distance between Brades Hall and Tividale. They served collieries, brickworks and quarries; the latter linked by tramway from workfaces high up on the Rowley ridge. Canalside at Tividale stood a large works manufacturing sheet iron which must have relied heavily on canal transport, there being no railway in proximity. It's

amazing how all this heavy industry has evaporated, most of this stretch of canal now being bordered by small industrial lockups or premises advertised optimistically as being available for let at favourable terms.

Blue-bricked and double-arched, Tividale Aqueduct spans the Netherton Branch which you first encountered back at Dudley Port Junction. Steps lead down to the lower level, from where it's worth walking along to the northern portal of Netherton Tunnel. The air at the entrance is cold and clammy, seemingly wanting to suck you into the gloomy bore built in 1858 to relieve the nearby Dudley Tunnel, already riddled with subsidence. When built it was the eighth longest canal tunnel in Britain, measuring 3,027 yards. Nowadays (pending re-opening of Standedge Tunnel on the Huddersfield Narrow Canal), it's second only to Blisworth on the Grand Union in Northamptonshire. At one time this impressive, twin-towpathed tunnel was lit by electricity powered from a turbine from the upper level at Tividale Aqueduct.

Turn your back on the tunnel, pass under the aqueduct - noting the canal employees' cottages numbered in the BCN sequence - and make a beeline back to Dudley Port Junction. On the way you'll pass a working foundry, almost a thing of the past in the rapidly turning green, Black Country now.

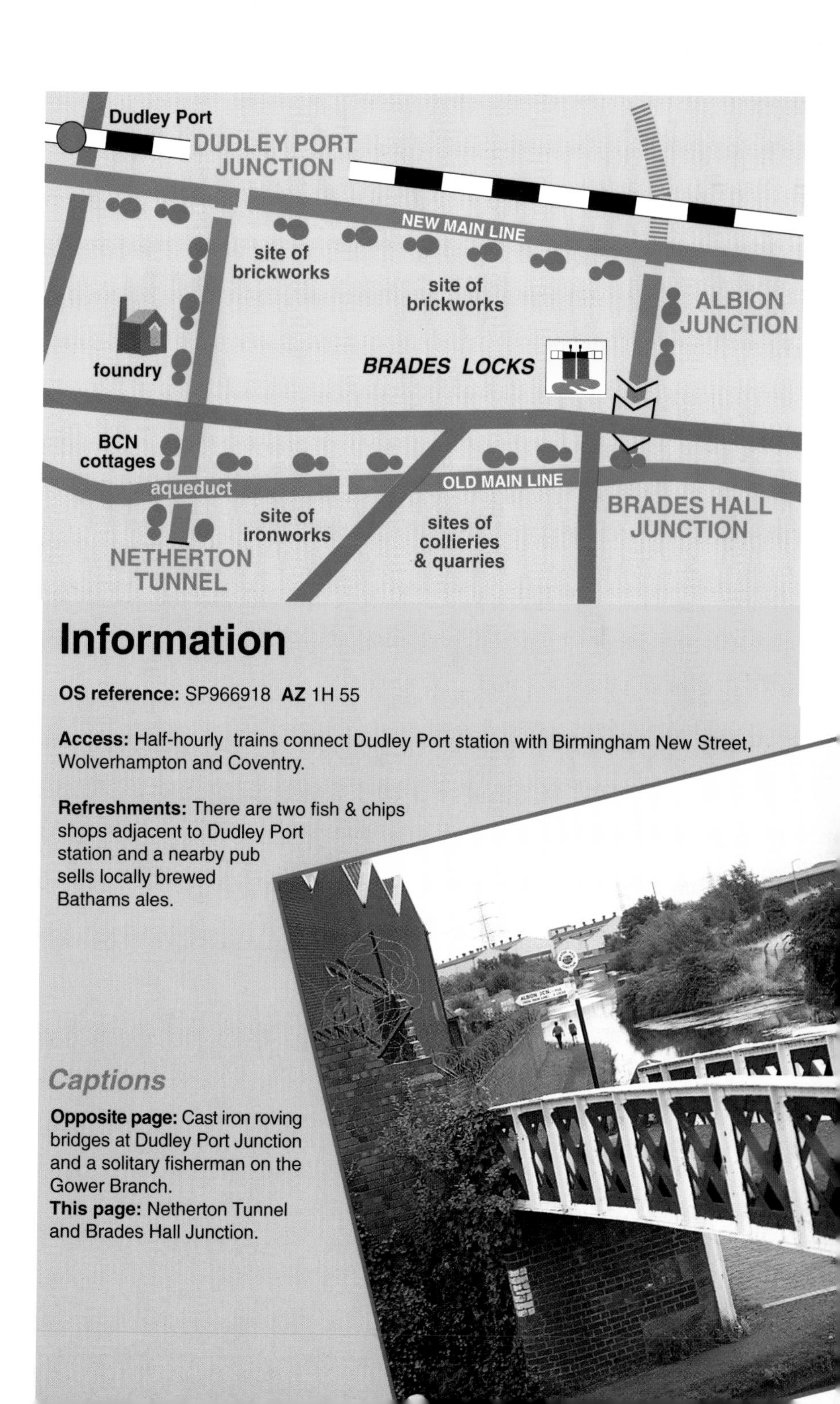

Information

OS reference: SP966918 **AZ** 1H 55

Access: Half-hourly trains connect Dudley Port station with Birmingham New Street, Wolverhampton and Coventry.

Refreshments: There are two fish & chips shops adjacent to Dudley Port station and a nearby pub sells locally brewed Bathams ales.

Captions

Opposite page: Cast iron roving bridges at Dudley Port Junction and a solitary fisherman on the Gower Branch.
This page: Netherton Tunnel and Brades Hall Junction.

THE BACK *of the* MAP

BETWEEN the Rowley Hills - the central ridge which divides the Black Country into two distinct parts - and the Stour Valley lies 'The Back of the Map', the name given by working boatmen to the Dudley and Stourbridge canals and their connecting branches. Here can be found some of the finest monuments to the golden age of canals, every bit as significant to posterity as the self-important Seven Wonders of the Waterways which, incidentally, cannot muster a BCN location between them.

There can be no better place to start exploring the 'Back of the Map' than Windmill End at Netherton, near Dudley. The fact that you need three names to pinpoint the location emphasises its low profile and, sadly, though you could once have arrived here by train - a little 'push & pull' affair which spent its days trundling between Old Hill and Dudley - the only public transport available now is the bus. But it's a pleasant experience to bounce down Withymoor Road on a number 412 bus from Cradley Heath, to alight at the Dry Dock, and to ascend the cinder path to Windmill End.

In canal terms Windmill End is defined by the junction of the Dudley No.2 Canal with the Netherton Branch, but the plot is delightfully thickened by the survival of a former loop in the canal which, when bypassed by improvements brought in the wake of the construction of Netherton Tunnel in 1858, was reduced to the status of two separate branches, known bluntly, but disarmingly, as the Boshboil and Bumble Hole arms.

A plethora of cast iron roving bridges, picked out in the traditional black and white colours of canal infrastructure, lend sparkle to the scene, straddling the divergent routes which make their entrances and exits into and out of an open landscape dominated by the ruin of an old engine house. This is Cobb's Engine House, perhaps the most potent post-industrial image in the whole of the Black Country. It dates from 1831 and the engine it once contained spent its working life of over a century pumping floodwater from neighbouring mines. The canal was not ungrateful for this water either, it helped maintain levels on a pound of extraordinary length, stretching from Tipton to Blower's Green, Birmingham, Selly Oak, Tardebigge and Lapworth.

The Ordnance Survey six inch map of 1904 shows that coal mining was already on the wane, but Warren's Hall Colliery was still sending coal down by incline to the sizeable basin still intact to the east of the junction. Other tramways were conveying stone from an assortment of quarries on the Rowley ridge. Other industrial activities clearly depicted on the map include brick and tile works, sawmills, foundries, a pottery and a boiler works, and you find yourself longing for the invention of a time machine which would facilitate a visit to early 19th century Netherton. Nowadays they hold regular boat rallies at Windmill End and there's a Bumble Hole Visitor Centre dedicated to the interpretation of the area's busy past.

Left: Toll End Works side bridge over the Boshboil Arm at Windmill End, with Cobb's Engine House in the background.

It's two miles by towpath from Windmill End to Park Head, a worthwhile walk encompassing the remains of a railway interchange basin at Withymoor, the site of Noah Hingley's Ironworks were the anchors for the *Titanic* were cast, a BCN reservoir and the roving bridge which marks the junction of the ill-fated Two Locks Line, a short cut rendered unnavigable by subsidence. Or you can cut across the hill via Netherton, passing the churchyard where 19th century cholera victims were consigned to mass, unmarked graves. But however you arrive, Park Head is another significant piece in the assembly of the 'Back of the Map' jigsaw. It marks the junction of the Dudley No.1 and Dudley No.2 canals.

As befits its numerical superiority, the Dudley No.1 Canal is the senior partner at Park Head. It opened in 1779, forging a through route, in association with the Stourbridge Canal, between the Staffordshire & Worcestershire Canal and the Birmingham Canal. Its most significant item of engineering was Dudley Tunnel, a 3154 yards long bore beneath the borough of Dudley itself; an extraordinary tunnel, riddled with subterranean limestone workings - see The Black Country Museum & Dudley Tunnel.

The Dudley No.2 Canal dates from 1798 and was built to take pressure off Dudley Tunnel and to avoid the high tolls being charged by the BCN at Tipton. The plan was to link with the Worcester & Birmingham at Selly Oak (see Cross City Connections), a daring route which included the construction of the fourth longest tunnel in Britain at Lapal.

Right: Looking down Park Head Locks, through an arch of the former Oxford, Worcester & Wolverhampton Railway's viaduct, towards the pumping house now used by Dudley Canal Trust as an information centre. Netherton church tower peeps over the trees on the horizon.

THE BACK of the MAP

Top of the Delph

There are four locks at Park Head, though originally there were five, the bottom two being combined into Blower's Green Lock at the end of the 19th century. At twelve feet, it's the deepest chamber on the BCN, and an increasingly used one, because the route from Dudley Port to Stourton is a popular short cut for the 'Stourport Ring' cruising circuit and holidaymakers, as opposed to diehard enthusiasts, are nowadays frequent travellers through this part of the Black Country. It must be a sobering experience, for those who hail from Haselmere, Horsham and Harrow, to expose themselves to the likes of Baptist End, Blower's Green and Brettell Lane.

Blower's Green Lock is overlooked by an imposing pumping house of similar design to the one on Brasshouse Lane, Smethwick, though this one's built of blue Staffordshire bricks. It houses an information centre operated by the Dudley Canal Trust - Tel: 01384 236275. The other three locks don't see much use on account of the restricted dimensions of Dudley Tunnel which preclude all but the lowest of craft from entering it. But it's an entertaining walk up the flight, past the former toll house and employee's cottage, beneath a viaduct of an abandoned railway and on to the top lock, above which there was once an intriguing three-way junction with the Grazebrook Arm (to the right) and Lord Ward's Pensnett Canal (on the left). You can carry on to inspect the southern portal of Dudley Tunnel (and be astonished at how small it seems compared to Netherton's), then return to Park Head Junction and consider where next to wend your way on the Back of the Map.

Not much more than a mile to the south lies Merry Hill, a name now synonymous with shopping, but, until 1983, the site of the massive Round Oak Steel Works. The blast furnaces have been replaced by shopping malls and office blocks and one comes to the inescapable conclusion that the Dudley Canal, in common with much of the BCN, has been emasculated in the process. This is not a place to linger if you have any enthusiasm for canal tradition and heritage.

Make tracks, then, for The Delph, an altogether more inspiring canalscape, an uncompromised 19th century masterpiece consisting of eight locks raising or lowering the Dudley No.1 Canal by eighty-five thrombotic feet. Six of these locks

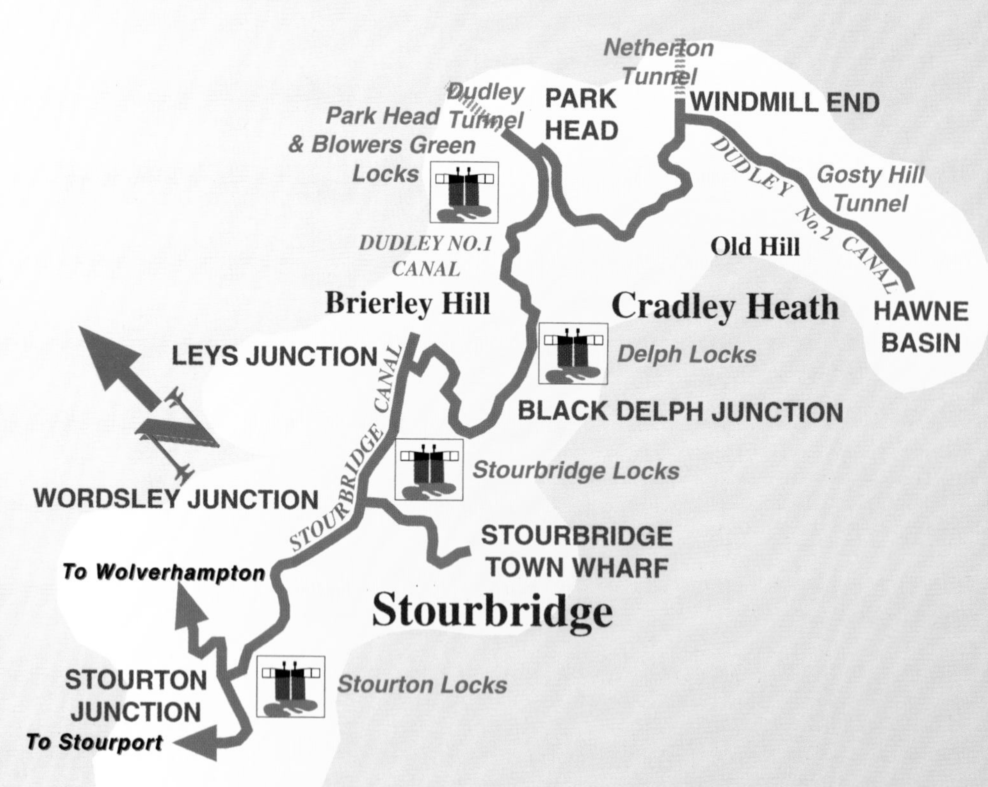

are in dramatic proximity and are accompanied by a sequence of overflow weirs, apt to cascade spectacularly when water levels are high. These six locks date from a rebuilding programme of 1858 which eradicated the original flight of seven, though something of its course can still be discerned, notably between the seventh and eighth locks up where a roving bridge spans the original line of the locks, now reduced to a reedy arm. The lock-keeper here nowadays has an abiding passion for the golden age of Hollywood cowboys. He occupies part of a former canal horse stable block also leased by the Birmingham Canal Navigations Society and occasionally opened to the public.

At the foot of Delph Locks, Black Delph Junction marks the meeting point of the Dudley No.1 and Stourbridge canals. Though closely linked, economically and historically, the Stourbridge Canal was never, unlike both Dudley canals, part of the BCN, remaining independently owned, and not a little profitable, until Nationalisation in 1948. It has its own flight of locks, no less than sixteen of them, ranged over a mile of canal between Leys and Wordsley junctions. The flight is at its most charismatic in the vicinity of Wordsley, where two significant buildings provide both historic and photogenic interest and appeal. The more vertically dominant of the two is the Red House Cone, sole survivor of a family of such kilns which once filled the Stourbridge skyline. Glass-making, especially crystal, has been a facet of the local economy since Huguenot refugees settled in the district in the 17th century. The advent of the canal, opened in 1779, boosted the glass industry, enabling coal to be brought in more cheaply. A fine 'silver' sand, an important ingredient in the manufacture of crystal, was carried here by boat from sand pits on the Grand Junction Canal in the vicinity of Leighton Buzzard.

The towpath rises to cross a former arm opposite the glassworks which once served a brass foundry. Alongside the next lock up stands an intriguing timber building of some size known as Dadford's Shed. Thomas Dadford was the engineer responsible for the design and construction of the Stourbridge Canal, slightly confusingly, because his father, also called Thomas, built the Dudley No.1 Canal. The eponym is posthumous, because this transhipment shed is late 19th century in its construction, which appears to defy perspective in that it tapers to the north-east. Its long canopy, supported by cast iron columns, gives protection to boats moored in the adjoining side basin. Nowadays these are mostly traditional craft being maintained and repaired by a specialist team of boatbuilders. In past times the shed handled goods for a nearby corn and seed mill and a local brewery. At one time it was used by Bantocks, agents for the Great Western Railway.

You'll find it difficult to resist further exploration of the Stourbridge flight. Above the next lock up the canal widens and a brick roving bridge spans entrance to a reedy side pond and former basin overlooked by an attractive general store known as 'The Dock'. Once there was a smithy and a stable block here. The basin was used as an assembly point for boats waiting to use a drydock which once stood on the opposite bank of the canal: so much history, you see, if you but scratch the surface! The next two locks were built originally as a 'staircase' sharing a common middle gate, but this was time-consuming to use and

Left: Classic view down the Stourbridge Sixteen with the Red House Cone and Dadford's Shed dominating the middle distance. The tug is *Nansen*, owned and restored by British Waterways, and a regular at local boat rallies.

Above: View up Stourbridge Locks.
Right: Stourbridge Ironworks.
Opposite page: Beguiling countryside west of Wordsley Junction.

wasteful of water supplies and was rebuilt, sometime in the middle of the 19th century as two conventional chambers separated by a tiny pound. A graceful, cantilevered bridge, with wrought iron railings, and a split to let the towrope of horse-drawn boats pass through, adds to the character of the scene, as do the cream-washed lock house and neighbouring poplar trees, another extremely photogenic grouping as depicted in the accompanying photograph.

At the foot of Stourbridge Locks, a branch sets off from Wordsley Junction, and makes its winding way into the centre of Stourbridge, a mile and a half away. A regular trip-boat operates along this interesting branch, so you might well be able to enjoy it afloat. But even simply on foot, there is much to see and admire. Look out for the old Dial glass works by Chubbs Bridge, and Coalbourn Brook Bridge which used to carry the Kinver Light Railway across the canal, a delightful 3ft 6ins gauge electric tramway which linked Amblecote with the popular tourist destination of Kinver Edge between 1901 and 1930. The final bend in the branch takes you past Stourbridge Iron Works where the first steam locomotive to run in North America was built. Appropriately enough, it was called the *Stourbridge Lion*, and it first ran in Pennsylvania in 1829. The iron works was founded in 1798 and still functions. Two side bridges span erstwhile arms into the premises; one, charmingly made of cast iron and pictured below, is dated 1873 and sports the name of the owner, John Bradley.

The end of the branch is presided over by a marvellously restored bonded warehouse, a real gem used now as a community centre, but was once where imported goods liable to excise duty were stored 'in bond' until claimed and paid for. The ground floor dates from 1799, the two upper floors (which overhang the original) being supported by some hefty cast iron columns. Also intact are the handsome and not unsubstantial Stourbridge Canal Company offices, located on cobbled Canal Street, and appropriately used now by the Stourbridge Navigation Trust. At one time the canal continued beneath High Street to an interchange basin with the Great Western Railway.

Information

WINDMILL END

OS reference: SO954882 **AZ** 1F 69
Access: Nearest station Cradley Heath, connections by bus number 412
Refreshments: The "Dry Dock" lies just beneath the canal embankment by Windmill End Junction. Eccentric decor but good food.

PARK HEAD

OS reference: SO934888 **AZ** 5C 54
Access: Nearest station Cradley Heath, connections by bus number 247 (ask for Cinder Bank and walk down Peartree Lane).
Refreshments: You'll have to leg it to Dudley or Merry Hill to find anything at all!

DELPH LOCKS

OS reference: SO920867 **AZ** 4A 68
Access: Nearest station Stourbridge Town, connections by bus number 297.
Refreshments: Lots of pubs nearby, but look no further than "The Vine" (aka Bull & Bladder) on Delph Road which is Batham's brewery tap and one of the finest and most traditional of Black Country pubs.

STOURBRIDGE SIXTEEN

OS reference: SO895866 **AZ** 4E 67
Access: Nearest station Stourbridge Town, connections by bus numbers 256/7.
Refreshments: Dock Stores & Off Licence by Lock 10.

STOURBRIDGE ARM

OS reference: SO899848 **AZ** 1F 83
Access: 10 minutes walk from Stourbridge Town railway station.
Refreshments: The "Moorings Tavern" is a cosy local backing on to the town Wharf. Many other cafes, restaurants and pubs in Stourbridge town centre within 5 minutes walk.

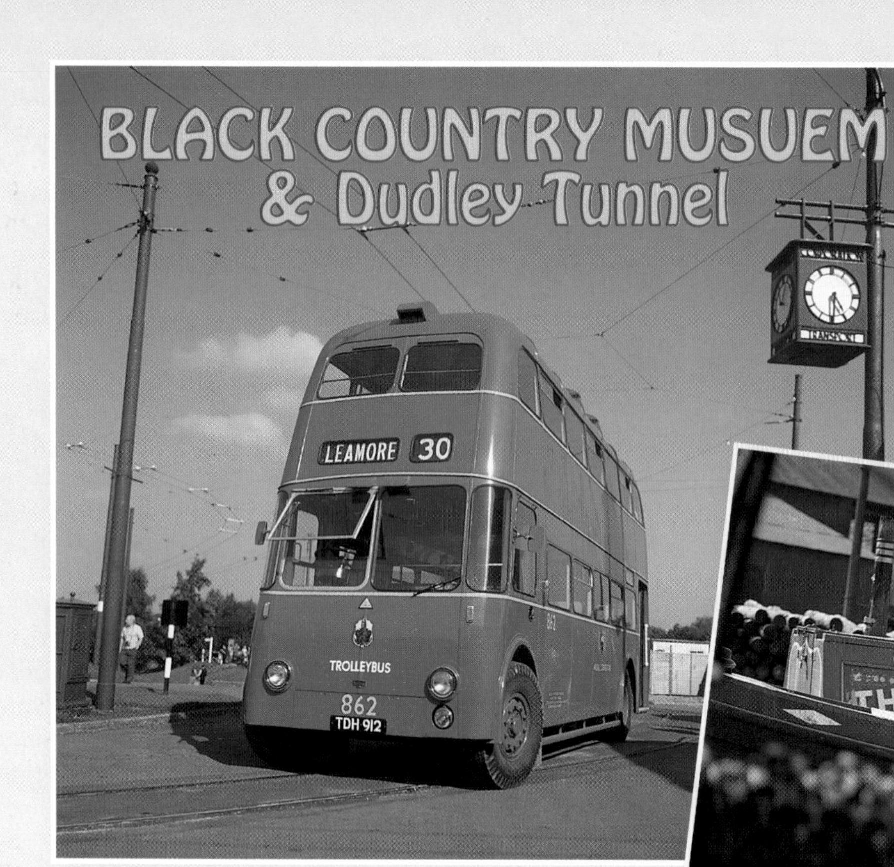

TEN years ago you could be forgiven for wondering what the point of the Black Country Museum was. The sort of businesses and buildings it was intent on preserving were still to be found throughout the Black Country. But the flannel cloth of Progress is wiping clean the face of the Black Country and redevelopment is riding it of many structures of character and historic significance, and so the work of the Black Country Museum becomes more and more valuable as time goes by.

It was difficult to resist headlining this feature with a Walsall Trolleybus - a Black Country built Sunbeam - they disappeared about the same time as the last traffics on the BCN and were synonymous with a number of the roadways paralleling or crossing the northern waters of the BCN.

But it is really with the museum's Boat Dock that this book is concerned. The museum site adjoins the northern portal of Dudley Tunnel and the branch which runs into the museum itself was originally known as Lord Ward's Canal and was constructed specifically to reach the massive lime kilns which are still to be found at its end.

The arm reaches into the museum beneath a typical BCN roving bridge followed by a spectacularly atypical vertical lift bridge rescued from the nearby Bloomfield Railway Basin. Beyond this lies a reconstructed boat dock of marked similarity to the many small yards which existed in various locations up and down the BCN network. Here, many of the traditional aspects of boat-building are still practised for the edification of visitors, and the museum is also playing an important role in passing down skills from generation to generation. A number of historic boats are usually on site. Craft such as *Stour,* the Thomas Clayton liquid carrying boat, *Birchills*, a typical 'joey' or day boat, and *Diamond* , a Midland & Coast butty painstakingly restored to its former glory.

The arm continues at a sharp right angle past the museum's forge and rolling mill then passes under Broad Street Bridge, moved here from Wolverhampton. A huge bank of lime kilns lies beyond, at which point the canal terminates.

Title picture: Former Walsall trolleybus No.862.
Above: Preserved Thomas Clayton motor *Stour.*
Right: The Boat Dock, Black Country Museum.

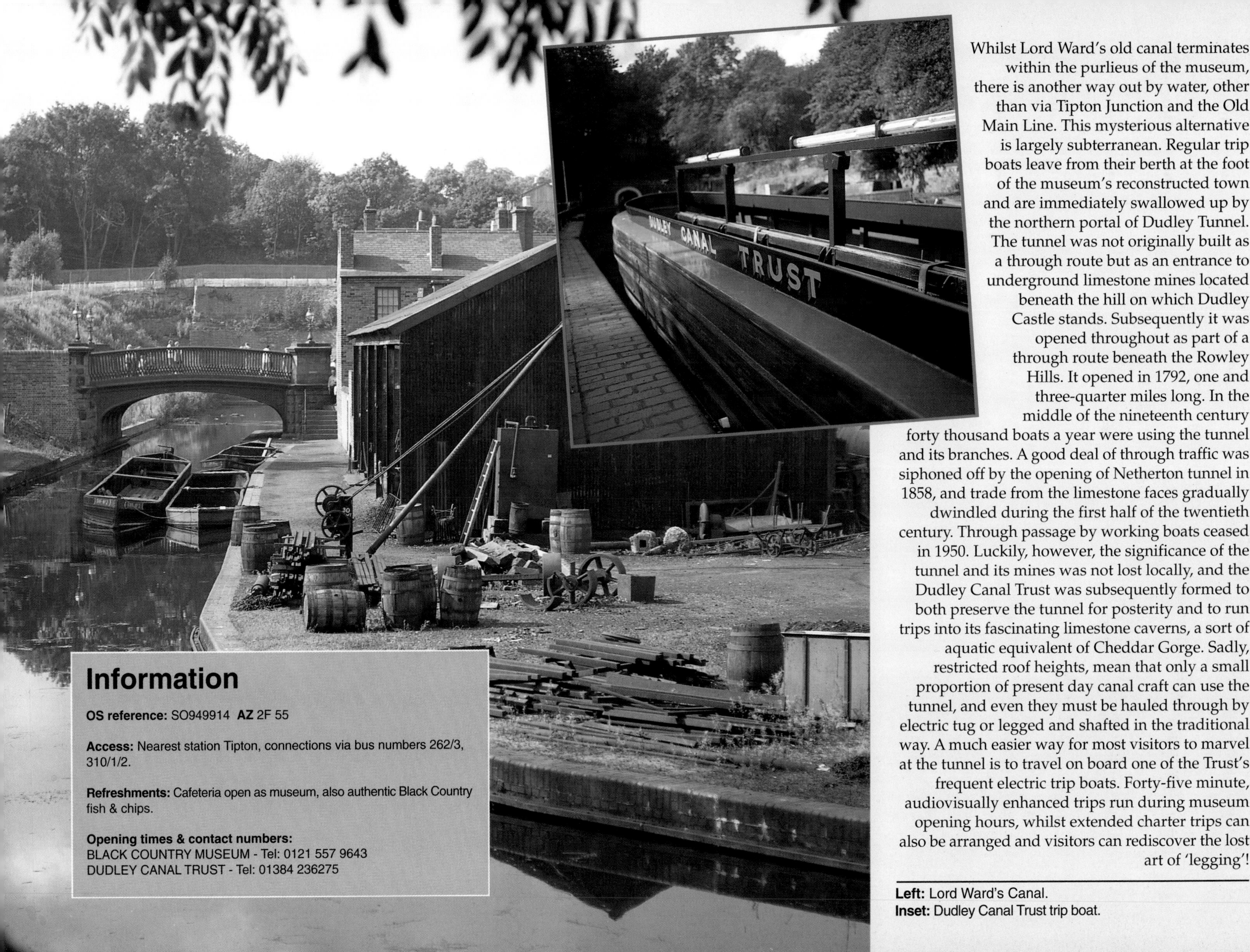

Whilst Lord Ward's old canal terminates within the purlieus of the museum, there is another way out by water, other than via Tipton Junction and the Old Main Line. This mysterious alternative is largely subterranean. Regular trip boats leave from their berth at the foot of the museum's reconstructed town and are immediately swallowed up by the northern portal of Dudley Tunnel. The tunnel was not originally built as a through route but as an entrance to underground limestone mines located beneath the hill on which Dudley Castle stands. Subsequently it was opened throughout as part of a through route beneath the Rowley Hills. It opened in 1792, one and three-quarter miles long. In the middle of the nineteenth century forty thousand boats a year were using the tunnel and its branches. A good deal of through traffic was siphoned off by the opening of Netherton tunnel in 1858, and trade from the limestone faces gradually dwindled during the first half of the twentieth century. Through passage by working boats ceased in 1950. Luckily, however, the significance of the tunnel and its mines was not lost locally, and the Dudley Canal Trust was subsequently formed to both preserve the tunnel for posterity and to run trips into its fascinating limestone caverns, a sort of aquatic equivalent of Cheddar Gorge. Sadly, restricted roof heights, mean that only a small proportion of present day canal craft can use the tunnel, and even they must be hauled through by electric tug or legged and shafted in the traditional way. A much easier way for most visitors to marvel at the tunnel is to travel on board one of the Trust's frequent electric trip boats. Forty-five minute, audiovisually enhanced trips run during museum opening hours, whilst extended charter trips can also be arranged and visitors can rediscover the lost art of 'legging'!

Left: Lord Ward's Canal.
Inset: Dudley Canal Trust trip boat.

Information

OS reference: SO949914 **AZ** 2F 55

Access: Nearest station Tipton, connections via bus numbers 262/3, 310/1/2.

Refreshments: Cafeteria open as museum, also authentic Black Country fish & chips.

Opening times & contact numbers:
BLACK COUNTRY MUSEUM - Tel: 0121 557 9643
DUDLEY CANAL TRUST - Tel: 01384 236275

WOLVERHAMPTON
& The Twenty-one

IT'S at Wolverhampton, perhaps more than at any other location on the Black Country canals, that you yearn for the use of a time machine. You want it to be nineteen-fifty-something, for there to be trolleybuses gliding between the cast iron balustrades of Broad Street Bridge, for there to be narrowboats unloading aluminium ingots in the old Fellows Morton & Clayton wharf, for there to be a Palethorpes sausage van in the High Level siding, for a 'King' to be steaming down to Stafford Road for coaling up before the run back to Paddington, for a boat girl to be riding bareback down to Autherley to collect an upcoming butty, and for a Thomas Clayton motor to be backing stern-first down to the gasworks arm to pick up some crude

What would we trade in now for such sights? Our lap-tops, our CDs, our twenty-five television channels with nothing on? Are we obsessed with the past because the present is so unpalatable?

Decanted from your train at Wolverhampton station, you can muse on such matters as, turning sharp right out of the entrance foyer, and right again opposite the British Transport Police station, you drop down through the gloomy, vitreous-tiled subway which once led travellers to their connections at the Great Western Railway's Low Level station, a blue-brick building in the classical mould, mothballed and trackless now, as if awaiting a second coming. The subway emerges into an only slightly less gloomy gallery in which you should turn left to reach Wednesfield Road.

Turn left beneath the railway and, out of curiousity, poke your head beneath the archway into the cobbled courtyard of Broad Street Wharf where the wall still proudly advertises Fellows Morton & Clayton's canal carrying activities, even though the depot is now a nightclub; a change of use which somehow neatly defines all that has happened to the BCN.

Beat a sober retreat, cross Broad Street (when you can find a suitable gap in the traffic) and pass across the sward of grass to the Top Lock, still presided over by its keeper's cottage and neighbouring a small boatyard. Follow the towpath down the flight. The massive, corrugated-iron clad depot on your left was built by the GWR in 1935. Between locks 3 and 4 the canal doglegs beneath what was once the rival LMS railway line to Stafford and the North. Lock 5 is numbered in stone by its tail gates and dated 1862, perhaps it was rebuilt about this time, for it was originally constructed, of course, eighty years earlier. Wolverhampton's distinctively green and yellow coloured trolleybuses -

Title picture & opposite: Restored narrowboat *Atlas*. **Right:** Wolverhampton Top Lock.

nany built by the local firm of Guy - used
:o cross Cannock Road Bridge on their
way to the housing estates of Low Hill
and Bushbury.

Locks 6-8 lay alongside the Great
Nestern main line to Shrewsbury, mid
Nales and the Mersey. The trackbed is
now a public open space overlooked by
:he local authority's high chimnied
ncinerator. The rival railway routes
crossed the canal, and each other, between
ocks 11 and 12. It must have been heaven
:o be a train-spotter here in steam days
when, as *Pearson's Canal Companion:
Stourport Ring* so eloquently puts it: "the
best of Swindon and Crewe puffed
mperiously overhead."

A lengthy, blue-brick viaduct carries
:he Stafford line over the site of
Wolverhampton Gas Works. Until 1966,
Thomas Clayton's liquid carrying
narrowboats (like *Ribble* pictured overleaf)
would reverse down this part of the flight
or ease of access to the gasworks basin
which lay below Lock 14 at an oblique
angle to the main line.

In common with other lengthy, urban
ock flights, 'hobblers' were a feature of
:he Wolverhampton Twenty- One.
Hobblers were otherwise unemployed
men who, for a small consideration, would
help boat captains with the locks, both to
ease the load and speed up passage.
Strangely enough, though the working
boats are long gone, hobblers can still
occasionally be seen helping modern-day
eisure boaters up and down the flight -
for an index-linked consideration, of
course!

You can continue down the flight if
you wish, following it, as it grows more
rural in character, past Wolverhampton's
Race Course, and on down to Aldersley
unction and the bosky assignation of the
BCN with the Staffs & Worcs Canal. But

Opposite page: Mill Street Bridge, Wolverhampton, looking towards Horseley Fields Junction. **Above:** Thomas Clayton's *Ribble* carries crude tar from Wolverhampton gas works past Broad Street *c*1964. *(Mike Webb)* **Right:** The same location today with Chubbs old factory prominent above the side bridge spanning the Broad Street arm.

perhaps it's time to retrace your steps and see what happens, beyond Broad Street, in the opposite direction.

The old Broad Street Bridge has been sent to a retirement home in the Black Country Museum. It's hard to imagine its replacement ever finding a niche in a museum. One trusts there will never be a question mark over the future of Chubb's huge triangular works which dominates the view here like a giant slab of chocolate cake. Chubbs themselves have moved to more modern premises now but their old factory remains a visible reminder of Wolverhampton's fame as a lock and safe-making town.

Heading towards Birmingham, the canal passes through a tunnel beneath the driveway to the railway station. Particularly on gloomy days, it isn't always easy to tell when you've left the tunnel behind, because, beyond it, the canal negotiates a canyon of tall, dark factory buildings. Numerous arms once egressed from the main line, penetrating factories and foundries, mills and wharves, and doing a roaring trade. Nowadays the towpath is the haunt of fishermen and cyclists, the latter officially encouraged by British Waterways, who have rubber-stamped and sanctioned towpath cycling between Wolverhampton and Birmingham.

At Horseley Fields Junction the Wyrley & Essington Canal heads off on its long, winding journey past Wednesfield and Walsall to Brownhills and beyond. It's worth walking a few hundred yards along this canal to see the hefty, blue-brick side bridges which span abandoned arms and to look back at the arm, on the opposite bank, which gave access to a basin where the LMS Railway had a dock for maintenance of its boats. Some of the associated buildings were restored for light industrial use recently, but sadly it is difficult to see them particularly well on account of burgeoning vegetation at the entrance to the arm.

Meanwhile the main line weaves its way through a heavily industrialised

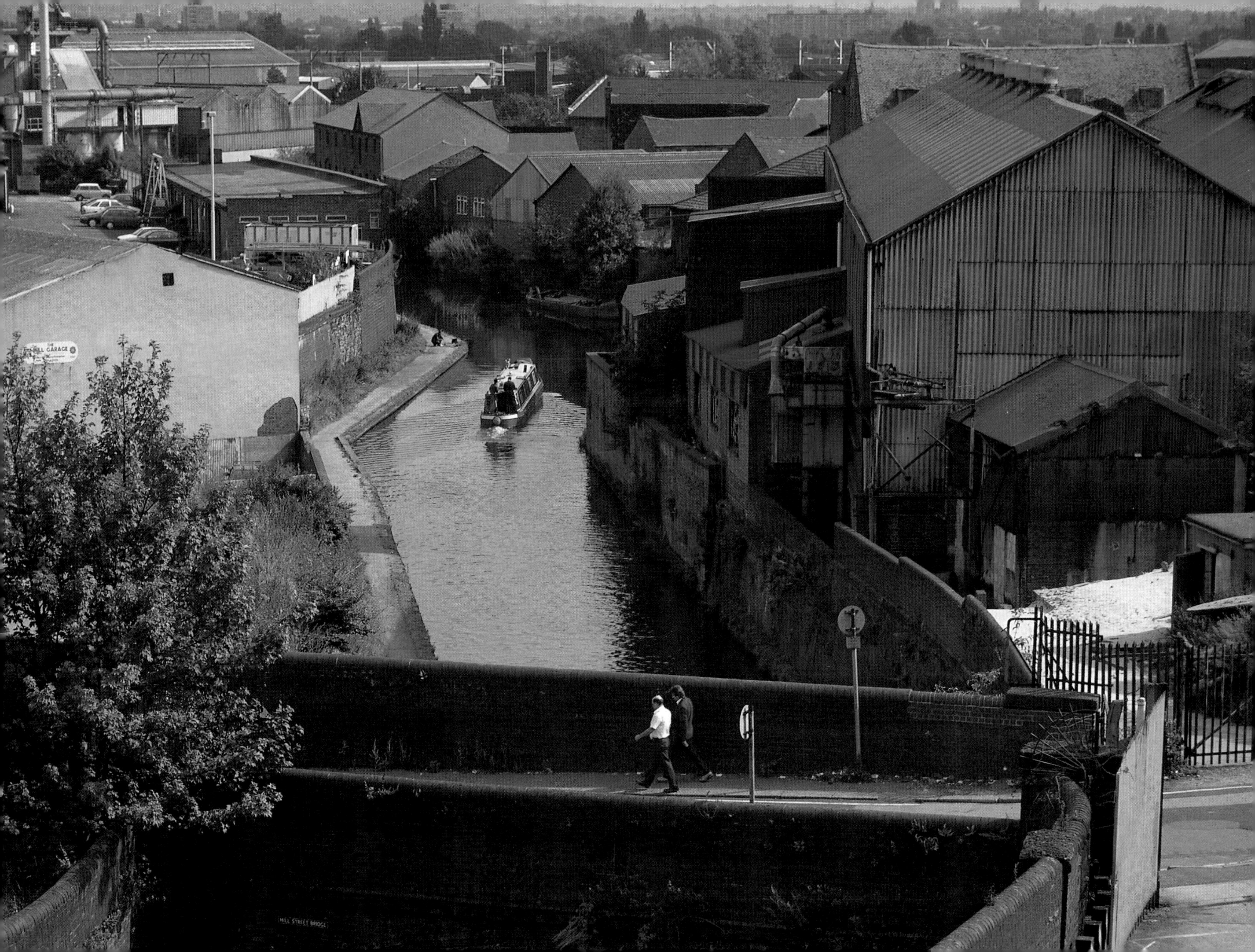
THE
GARAGE
MILL STREET BRIDGE

Left: Horseley Fields Junction seen from the Wyrley & Essington Canal.
Above: Chillington Wharf, now a listed structure.

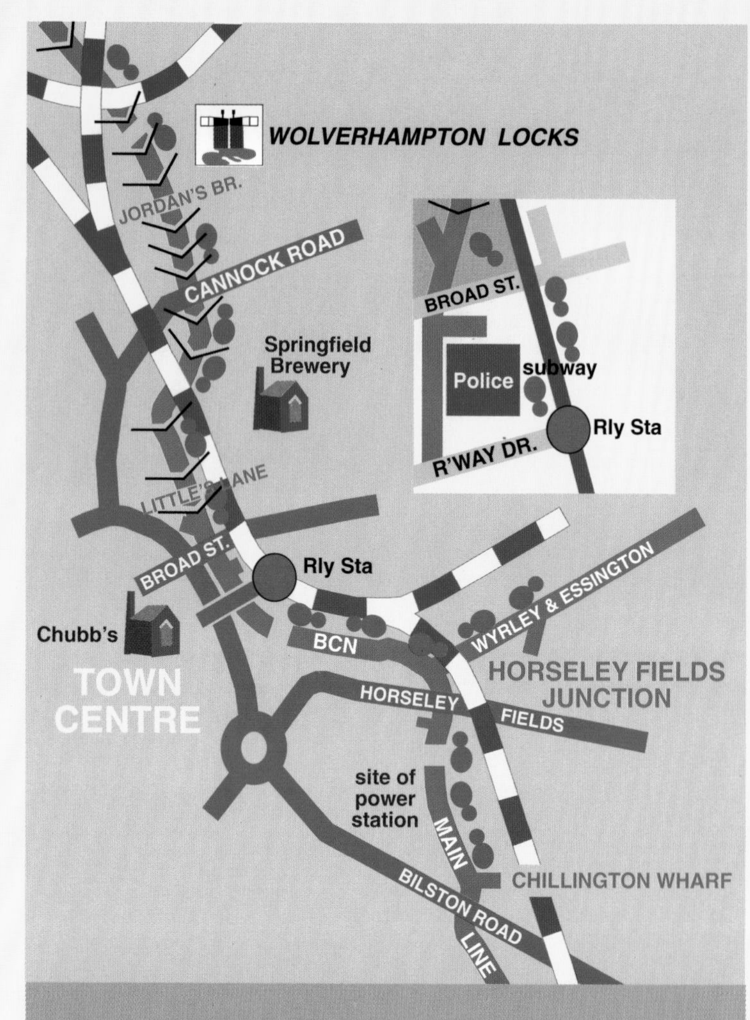

zone, albeit one which has turned its back on the canal. Often there will be some signs of boatbuilding activity at Minerva Wharf. Reference to old, large scale maps will help you unravel some of the mysteries of past activity. Notably, there was an ironworks, another railway basin - this one belonging to the Great Western and located more or less where BOC go about their business now - and, perhaps most significantly in terms of canal trade, the premises of Wolverhampton's power station which devoured many a ton of Cannock coal brought in by day boats known, colloquially, as 'joeys'. Parts of the generating plant stubbornly remain intact, but the unloading gantries and apparatus have disappeared with the boats themselves. Not much further, however, along the towpath, you'll come upon one of the most significant survivals on the BCN network. This is Chillington Wharf (aka Monmore Green) a more or less whole railway basin which once belonged to the London & North Western. In the commercial heyday of the BCN there were more than forty such interchange basins operated by the LNWR, GWR and Midland Railway. Obviously, there is no longer any boating activity at Chillington Wharf, but the railway sidings are still used as part of Wolverhampton's increasingly profitable steel terminal operated by English Welsh & Scottish Railway. Finally, before returning to Broad Street via the towpath, pause to watch one of a new generation of rail based vehicles cross the canal. The wheel has, quite literally, turned full circle, trams are back on the streets of Wolverhampton!

Information

OS reference: SO919989 **AZ** 1A 30

Access: Frequent express and local trains connect Wolverhampton with Birmingham and Coventry.

Refreshments: Try the "Great Western" on Sun Street (turn right instead of left at the foot of the subway under the railway station) for its good food, locally brewed Bathams and Holdens beers, and GW railway memorabilia.

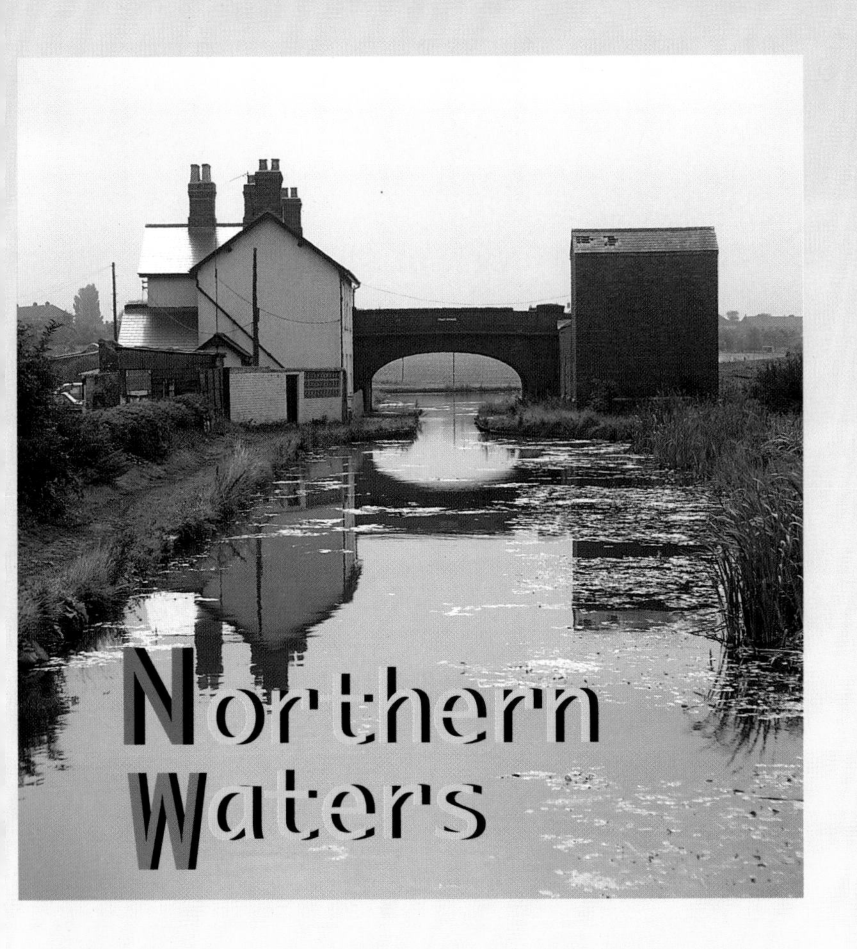

Northern Waters

BOATS are rarely encountered these days on the 'northern waters' of the Birmingham Canal Navigations. The likes of the Walsall, Wyrley & Essington and Tame Valley canals have yet to attract holidaymakers, and perhaps never will, being too far off the beaten track, both geographically and emotionally to ever become popular. There are ambitious plans to restore two lost links - with Lichfield and the Coventry Canal and Hatherton and the Staffordshire & Worcestershire Canal - which would recreate a fairly rural route across the top end of the BCN, the sort that hireboaters (the lifeblood of most canal routes these days) would be attracted to. But such a scheme would be years from fruition, and in the meantime an end of the world atmosphere hangs over these lugubrious waters; a challenge to the explorer in all of us.

Business was once brisk hereabouts, though. So brisk that there was a daily phenomenon known as the 'Black Country Tide', a bore brought about by the simultaneous movement of convoys of narrowboats, upwards of fifty at a time, converging on Pelsall Junction from Walsall and Brownhills. Their combined passage up the Cannock Extension Canal caused the water level to rise by half a foot; positively a tidal wave in canal terms. All these boats would be heading for the local collieries, to reload, before returning to the factories, foundries and power generating plants of the Black Country with vital supplies of coal. It wasn't only the industrialists who wanted the black stuff. A good proportion of it 'went missing' on its way through the housing estates of Bloxwich, Walsall Wood and Wednesfield. Whether out of fear, or more probably indifference, steerers turned a blind eye to pilferers who would board a passing boat at one bridge-hole, fill a sack of coal and depart at the next with their booty. Times were hard and houses had to be heated. Respectable women with families to feed were driven, often with their husband's consent, to sell themselves on the towpath to make ends meet.

Trade evaporated from these canals in the mid nineteen sixties. Artificially prolonged by the petrol rationing of the Second World War, canal transport gave way to the ubiquitous lorry and government sponsored road improvement schemes that the canal infrastructure, unchanged for a century, just couldn't compete with. The Cannock coalfield was in decline too, as soon would be, the region's traditionally heavy industries. Large chunks of the canal network were abandoned: the Cannock Extension Canal beyond Norton Canes, the Wyrley & Essington beyond Ogley Junction; the Bentley Canal and the Bradley Branch were all strategic links in the BCN system rendered unnavigable in the Sixties. We must be grateful for what survived and the atmosphere it continues to evoke.

This northern territory of the BCN - 'The Backwoods' working boatmen used to call it - retains

Title picture: Friar Bridge, Cannock Extension Canal. Former employees cottages on left, former stables on right.
Below: Looping the loop, Anglesley Basin.

an air of remoteness about it, in spite of its location in a conurbation of three million people. One of the most rewarding areas to explore is in the neighbourhood of Pelsall and Brownhills where the topography of various canal routes almost forms a perfect circuit for towpath walking.

So get yourself to Brownhills by bus, armed with OS Landranger Map 139 and a copy of *Pearson's Stourport Ring Canal Companion*. Join the canal at the bottom of the retail market, cross the footbridge and follow the towpath to Catshill Junction. Cross the roving bridge here and, remaining on the route of the Wyrley & Essington Canal, make your way to Ogley Junction. Until its abandonment in 1954, the W&E continued east from here in the direction of Lichfield. A typical cast iron roving bridge spans the course of the main line. A small marina occupies the remaining stub in water. One looks forward to full restoration.

The next part of your journey takes you along the Anglesey Branch. Originally built as a feeder from Chasewater Reservoir, opened in 1800 to bring much needed water supplies to the Wyrley & Essington, the branch was upgraded to navigable status to serve newly sunk collieries in the district. The coal trade survived up until 1967. Remnants of the loading apparatus still stand beside the water where the canal widens into an almost lake-like terminal basin at the foot of the Chasewater Reservoir's dam. Disappointingly, the lonely, heathland countryside surrounding the basin, which enjoys the status of a site of special scientific interest, is threatened by construction of the Birmingham Northern Relief road. The moral is: 'get there soon!'

Using your map or guidebook, find your way across the Watling Street (A5) and over Wyrley Common to the Cannock Extension Canal. Originally almost six miles long, this canal ran between Pelsall and Hednesford. It was opened in 1863 to tap the Cannock coalfield.
Ironically, coal was the canal's downfall too, the top four miles being abandoned because of subsidence in 1963; though by this time most of the Cannock area's coal was being transported by rail in any case. There was a link at Bridgtown, on the A5 near Cannock, with the Staffordshire & Worcestershire Canal's Hatherton Branch, another potential candidate for restoration. The connection was formed by a precipitous flight of thirteen locks, subsequently obliterated by opencast mining; a tough proposition for would be restorers.

Meanwhile we must be grateful for the two miles of the Cannock Extension still extant, especially as it represents possibly the last significant essay in narrowbeam canal construction in this country. It has considerable character, running absolutely straight across a rural landscape hard to associate with the heartlands of the BCN. Follow the towpath down past stagnant ponds to Pelsall Junction where former canal horse stables and a pair of old canal workers' cottages rekindle the atmosphere of working boat times. Look around you at the pock-marked wasteland and marvel that there was once a flourishing ironworks here and a colliery too.

It's a two mile walk back to Brownhills along the Wyrley & Essington, living up to its nickname, the 'Curley Wyrley'. Lots of old arms lurk in the undergrowth, and there are two former railway bridges encountered on the way. You are not only walking along a towpath somewhere in the West Midlands, you are walking through time itself!

Above: Late harvest, Ogley Junction.
Opposite: *Diamond* joins the Wyrley & Essington Canal at Pelsall Junction.

Redevelopment of the Black Country has altered the character of the Walsall Canal to a greater extent than possibly any other BCN constituent. After many years of moribund dereliction, Walsall's Town Wharf is being redeveloped. Already a smart new pub has opened its doors to an appreciative public and, in 1999, a new art gallery will follow. Recreation is the arm's future, its past was anything but. Here in the old days there might have been as many as fifty boats at a time loading and unloading along the arm. Many of the incoming cargoes would have been worked from ports on the Severn or the Mersey. For many years vital supplies of Guinness stout were carried by boat along the Shropshire Union from Ellesmere Port. They were nicknamed the nigger boats because of the beer's dark colour. Not all the beer which left Dublin would arrive at Walsall. There would be a degree of 'seepage' from the barrels, its absence disguised by the introduction of canal water. No wonder British Guinness has always had a reputation of tasting different to its Irish counterpart.

So, once upon a time the Walsall Arm would have been a thriving inland port. Gradually, however, as trade was lost to the railways and then the road, its wharves became disused. In the last years of dwindling trade, there were more tramps than boats. The homeless gravitated here at night to find some residual warmth amidst the discarded ash piles of a canalside foundry.

Nowadays, after years of being abandoned due to instabilities caused by subterranean limestone workings, the arm has been rewatered and is being refurbished. Pleasure boats come occasionally, usually in the safety of numbers that a convoy brings, for the canal journey to reach Walsall is still fraught with overtones of vandalism and made difficult by high levels of flotsam and jetsam in the cut.

At the outer end of the arm there's a T junction offering canal travellers, afoot or afloat, a choice of directions: left along the Walsall Canal to Darlaston, Great Bridge and, eventually, Birmingham; or right up the Walsall Junction Canal's flight of eight locks which will take you to Wolverhampton or Brownhills. Even by BCN standards the 'Walsall Eight' are imbued with melancholy. Boats are a rare commodity. The flight is numbered from the top. Number eight is islanded by wasteground. Number seven is overlooked by the handsome facade of Albion Mill, erected in 1849, and still producing flour. Alongside the lock is an arched loading bay, but naturally, or rather unnaturally, everything goes out in cream coloured road tankers now. On the towpath side a brick built side bridge straddles the entrance to an old dock which may have been used to store boats waiting to unload at the mill, though there was also an ironworks in the vicinity which may have made use of it. Lock 6, unusually, has mitred bottom gates, wheras the rest of the flight are in the more common single leaf BCN style.

A road bridge, overlooked by a somewhat sullen church, separates locks 4 and 5.

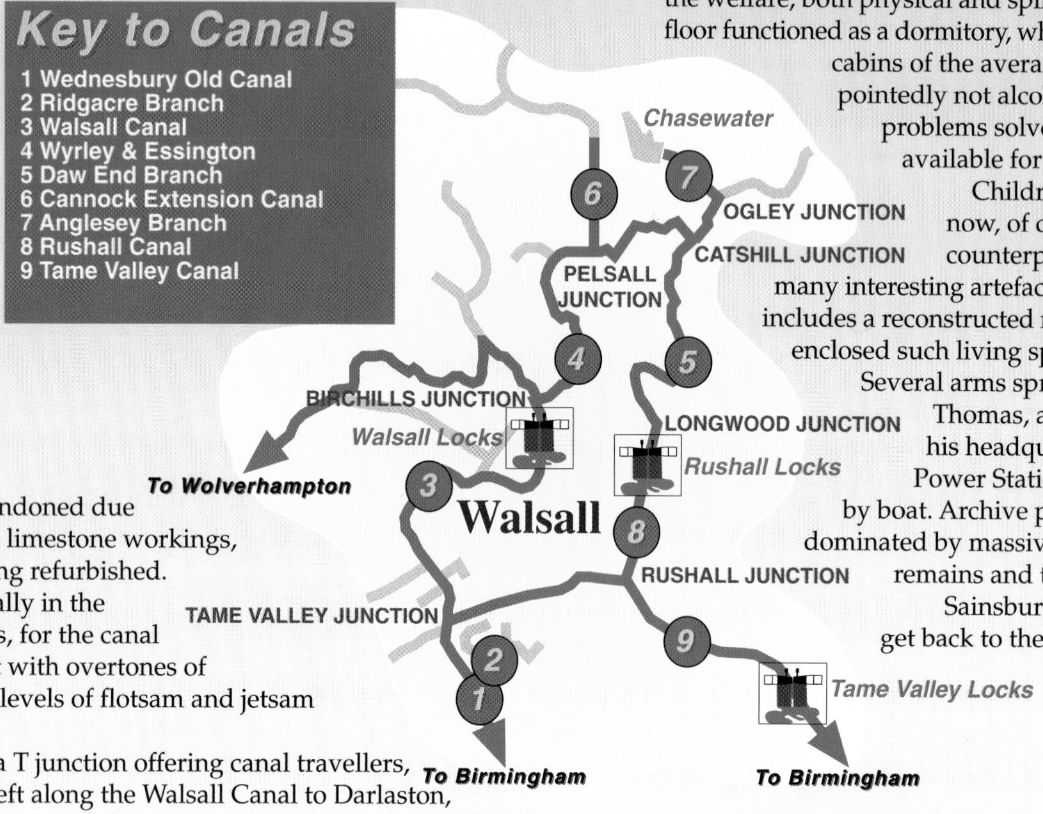

Key to Canals

1 Wednesbury Old Canal
2 Ridgacre Branch
3 Walsall Canal
4 Wyrley & Essington
5 Daw End Branch
6 Cannock Extension Canal
7 Anglesey Branch
8 Rushall Canal
9 Tame Valley Canal

A glimpse is caught of Christ on the cross before the bridgehole swallows you up. With terraced housing on one side, and long-grassed wastegrounds on the other, the canal ascends to the top lock and a building of much historical significance on the BCN. Now used, appropriately as a small museum devoted to interpretation of the history of the canals of the Walsall area, this neat, redbrick, two storey building was built in 1900 by the Seamen & Boatmen's Friendly Society to care for the welfare, both physical and spiritual, of the area's working boatmen. The upper floor functioned as a dormitory, which presumably made a change from the Spartan cabins of the average day boat. Downstairs, refreshments - though pointedly not alcohol! - were freely available, letters were written, problems solved, and there was even a modicum of education available for the children of boating families.

Children still come here in educational groups, but now, of course, to learn of the austere life of their counterparts a century ago. The museum contains many interesting artefacts garnered from neighbouring canals, and even includes a reconstructed narrowboat cabin to give visitors an idea of how enclosed such living spaces could be.

Several arms sprouted from the canal above the top lock. Ernest Thomas, a well known Black Country boat operator, had his headquarters here. Around the corner stood Birchills Power Station, a hungry consumer of local coal brought in by boat. Archive photographs reveal busy unloading scenes dominated by massive grabs and gantries. Only the roving bridge remains and the site has recently been redeveloped with a Sainsbury's supermarket as its centrepiece. You'd better get back to the Town Arm before nostalgic tears start to flow.

Information

Brownhills

OS reference: SK047053 **AZ** 2E 17

Access: Nearest station Walsall, connections by bus numbers 392-396.

Refreshments: The "Royal Oak" by Yorks Bridge near Pelsall Junction is a convivial canalside well thought of for its food.

Walsall

OS reference: SP012986 **AZ** 1G 33

Access: Nearest station Walsall. Frequent connections from Birmingham and Wolverhampton.

Refreshments: Try the swish new pub on Walsall Wharf.

Walsall Eight

Main Picture: Restored Associated Canal Carriers motor *Prince* leaves Lock 8, overlooked by the Albion Flour Mill.
Left inset: Looking up the flight from Lock 7.
Right inset: *Prince* leaves Lock 5.

CROSS CITY *connections*

CENTRO'S 'Cross-City' rail route links several canal locations of interest - facilitating many one-way walks. Here's a five mile suggestion, taking in the Worcester & Birmingham Canal - once famously described as "stretching its green fingers into the city" - the city centre canals of Gas Street Basin, Water's Edge and Cambrian Wharf, and the Birmingham & Fazeley Canal which heads eastwards out of Birmingham by way of two lengthy flights of locks.

Take the train from New Street to Selly Oak. Turn left outside the station on to Bristol Road. There's no access where it crosses the canal, so continue for a couple of hundred yards then turn left (opposite Deep Pan Pizza) into The Dingle, a side road leading down to the towpath. Turn left and head towards the city centre.

If the history books didn't tell you that there was once a junction between the Worcester & Birmingham and Dudley No.2 canals at Selly Oak you wouldn't know it. The actual meeting place of the two routes lay between the road and railway bridges on the towpath side, but the roving bridge is long gone, and vegetation hides any hint of previous earthworks. The Lapal Canal Trust has long term ambitions of restoring this canal.

Passing beneath the railway, you're treated to a breathtaking view of Birmingham University and its Italianate clock tower, nicknamed 'Uncle Joe' by generations of students, after Joseph Chamberlain, an early benefactor of the Edwardian campus. The Worcester & Birmingham towpath is popular with students for running and as a short cut for cycling into the city.

This section of canal was built in 1795, but it was another twenty years before the route opened throughout between Birmingham and Worcester. The parallel railway was opened in 1876 as the Birmingham West Suburban line. Unlike the canal, it still fulfils its original purpose of bringing thousands of commuters into the city each day. Both routes have short tunnels at Edgbaston; the canal's is towpathed and lighted and measures 105 yards in length.

This really is the most pleasant of ways to approach the centre of Birmingham, which delays exerting its urban influence until the last possible moment. It was this green, sylvan back door into Birmingham which caused Robert Aickman, founder of the Inland Waterways Association to quote, memorably, about canals stretching green fingers into towns.

"Beer at Home" no longer "Means Davenports", whose canalside brewery near Five Ways has been replaced by flats. By Bridge 88 a former council works depot enjoys a new lease of life as an antiques and crafts centre. Beyond here the canal turns left at ninety degrees. This is Salvage Turn, so called because there was a refuse dock at this point. Narrow gauge tracks embedded in the towpath cobblestones give a clue to former activity here.

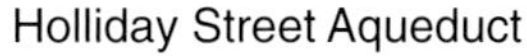

Holliday Street Aqueduct

Crossing Holliday Street on an elegant aqueduct (best appreciated from road level) the canal reaches Worcester Bar and Gas Street Basin. Frequently, in the early days of canal construction, new routes were perceived as rivals rather than potential additions to profit. The Birmingham Canal was worried that its precious water supplies would disappear down the fledgling Worcester & Birmingham into the River Severn and that its ally, the Staffordshire & Worcestershire, would lose trade to the new canal. Thus came into being the infamous Worcester Bar, a seven foot strip of land separating the two canals. For nearly twenty years cargoes were time-consumingly and expensively and frustratingly transhipped across the bar until common sense prevailed and a stop lock was inserted in 1815. The canal still narrows at this point, though the stop lock gates have gone and a neat little parody of a BCN cast iron bridge spans the junction of the two canals now, whilst the toll keeper's office has recently become a popular waterside cafe.

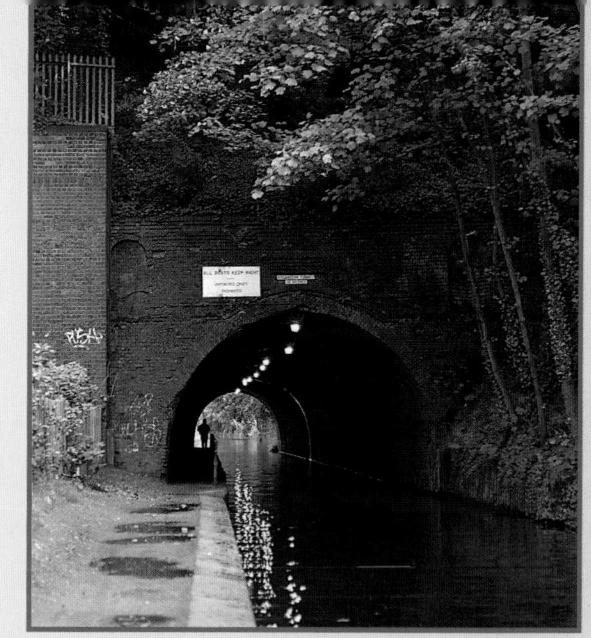

Edgbaston Tunnel

Nomenclature does not come much more utilitarian than Gas Street Basin. You are too late to see it in its workaday pomp - the working boats have gone, its warehouses were demolished in the Philistine Seventies and the original terminal arm into Suffolk Street ends abruptly in a brick wall - but enough remains to furnish you with cast iron clues to how things might have looked and a small community of residential boats add colour and life to an increasingly popular leisure area of the city.

The busy thoroughfare of Broad Street separates Gas Street from Water's Edge and the International Convention Centre. The canal effects this scene change by passing through a short tunnel, towpathed on either side. There used to be a Unitarian Church at street level with the apocryphal repute of baptising its congregation in the canal via a trapdoor in the roof of the tunnel.

Aston
Aston Locks
8
7
ASTON JUNCTION
Farmer's Bridge Locks
Snow Hill
6
City Centre
5
4
New Street
Five Ways
3
University
2
1
Selly Oak

KEY

1 Dudley No.2 Canal junction (site of)
2 University Campanile
3 Edgbaston Tunnel
4 Gas Street Basin
5 Water's Edge & ICC
6 Cambrian Wharf
7 Baker Bridge
8 Gasholders

Opposite page: The Worcester & Birmingham Canal runs past Birmingham University near Selly Oak.

Worcester Bar

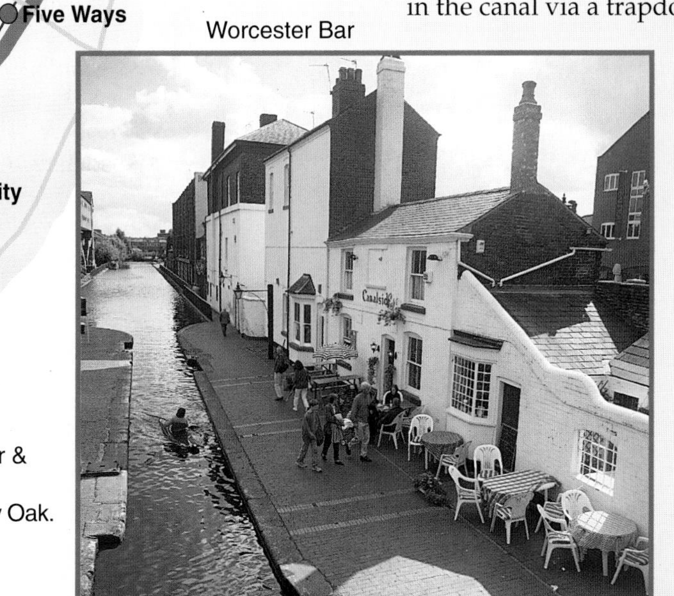

But it is the new religions of commerce and leisure which are symptomatic of central Birmingham's canalscape now. Goodness knows what the working boatmen and wharfingers of the past would make of Brindley Place and all its accoutrements: the cafes and restaurants, trip boats and waterbuses, and crowds of people with no visibly definable role other than that of bystanders, or 'gongoozellers', as they are known to the canal fraternity. Here are people, ensconced in restaurants, eating more for their lunch than a 19th century bargee might have expected to consume in a working week. As an onlooker, however, you cannot help but admire the transformation of the canal and its importance in creating the theme with which the ICC, the Water's Edge and Brindley Place all harmonise. Make no mistake, if the canal hadn't been a focal point, all this development could scarcely have succeeded so effectively.

Overlooked by the National Sea Life Centre and the National Indoor Arena, Old Turn Junction forms a pivotal point in Birmingham's canal network: the main line to Wolverhampton heads off eastwards, whilst the Birmingham & Fazeley Canal, merged with the Birmingham Canal Navigations in 1794, leaves in the opposite direction, passing Cambrian Wharf before negotiating an atmospheric flight of thirteen locks which act as a sort of aquatic boundary between Birmingham's commercial district and the Jewellery Quarter. Until 1926, the basin at Cambrian Wharf continued as the Newhall Branch serving further wharves closer to the city centre. These days the 'Old Thirteen', as the Farmer's Bridge locks are often referred to, work their way down through an area of student flats and design studios, burrowing beneath the Telecommunications Tower and the reactivated Snow Hill railway station before daylight is rediscovered in the vicinity of Aston Junction.

By Birmingham standards, this stretch of canal is busy with boats, and it is unusual, in the summer months at any rate, to walk its towpath without meeting at least one crew grappling with the arduous task of lock operation. Even at a sauntering pace, it should take you no more than forty-five minutes to amble from Old Turn to Aston Junction, by boat, through all those locks, you could be looking at three hours.

Old Turn Junction with gongoozling Canada geese

Time, however, is not necessarily of the essence in canal circles. Most boaters will be only too happy to rest their bottoms on a balance beam and regale you with heroic tales of flights climbed, tunnels negotiated, miles covered, and prodigious amounts of rubbish extracted from their props. Likewise, you should take the time to soak up the atmosphere, to strike a notional balance line between past and present, an extrapolation of cause and effect in canal terms, of why this roving bridge should be here, and why that side pond should be there.

By the eleventh lock down, it's feasible to vault a low brick wall into Ludgate Hill, and to walk up to St Paul's Square, a patch of green, in an otherwise densely urbanised area, harbouring a handsome Georgian church of the same name. Meanwhile, back on the towpath, you pass into a huge blue-brick vault carrying Snow Hill station over the canal, trains rumbling over it again now after a period in the trackless wilderness of the Seventies and Eighties.

Beyond Snow Hill and the A41 road crossing, you sense an opening out of both the canal and the cityscape as a whole. Nevertheless, there were basins aplenty hereabouts, serving

Water's Edge and Symphony Hall

Snow Hill & Aston

Main picture: Canal vault beneath Snow Hill railway station.
Top left: Spectators at Farmer's Bridge locks.
Below left: Aston Top Lock.
Below right: Lovers at Lock 7, Aston flight.

Left: Factoryscape between locks 9 and 10 on the Aston flight.

sundry wharves, notably an electricity generating plant, chemical works, wire mill and a dispersal point for the noisome cargo euphemistically known as 'night soil' which would be taken for use as manure in country districts beyond the city's rim. Birmingham's General Hospital stood in the vicinity between 1779 and 1897.

Barker Bridge is named after William Barker, a North Staffordshire ironmaster who came to live in Birmingham in the mid 19th century. Somewhere down the years it has mislaid one of its ornamental arches. Beyond the next road bridge the towpath seesaws over a trio of side bridges which used to serve St Stephen's Wharf, a copper works and an iron works.

At Aston Junction the Digbeth Branch sets off, threading its way through the 21st century environs of Aston Science Park. The Birmingham & Fazeley Canal immediately plunges down the first of eleven locks which have a total rise or fall of seventy feet. By now you're beginning to leave fellow towpath-users behind, only ardent industrial archaeologists and joggers seem to venture this far. Redevelopment is gradually eroding much of the Aston flight's post industrial charm but an horizon full of gasholders still generates some semblance of heavy industry. Towards the foot of the flight the lock chambers are more spaced out. You should leave the towpath by the bottom lock, turn onto Holborn Hill and cross Lichfield road to Aston station. It'll take you six or seven minutes to get back to the city centre by train as opposed to five hours by boat - no wonder canal carrying is defunct!

Information

OS reference: SP044827. **AZ:** 3A 152

Access: Frequent trains connect Selly Oak station with Birmingham New Street and Aston.

Refreshments: Break your journey at Gas Street Basin where the "Canalside Cafe" will refuel you for the next leg. Alternatively, a wide choice of establishments cluster around Waters Edge and Brindley Place.

Renaissance

British Waterways

IF you'd plucked up the courage, to say, in the Seventies, that Birmingham's greatest asset was 'The BCN' - it's hundred mile network of industrially abandoned canals - you'd have been ridiculed, but you would have had the last laugh. And if you'd had the foresight to invest in canalside real estate, you might have had a fortune on your hands, for nowadays canal renaissance has redefined Birmingham and the Black Country as the place to go for innovative approaches to waterside regeneration.

Just add water, and watch, how canals, nationwide, have become a focal point for redevelopment and regeneration. Architects love to see their work reflected in water, and Birmingham and the Black Country have plenty of that lurking in lengths of canal, waiting to be rediscovered, reappraised and redefined into settings for 21st century expansion.

British Waterways, custodian's of the canal network throughout Britain, are at pains to achieve a sensitive melding of past and future resources, and are achieving this through key partnerships within the public, private and voluntary sectors. It is significant that time-honoured traditional skills are still employed in the upkeep of the canals. There are over four hundred locks in the West Midlands and their gates are still hand made in Tipton using procedures and methods which Brindley wouldn't bat an eye-lid at. Aqueducts and bridges are repaired with reclaimed bricks and heritage mortars mixed to match the original materials. Passed down through the generations, continued use of such skills ensures that the canal system remains recognisably 18th century in origin but functions for 21st century use.

Throughout Birmingham and the Black Country local communities play a pivotal role in canal regeneration. Where their predecessors eked out a living steering coal boats, or breaking ice to keep the channels clear, modern-day West Midlanders use the system for leisure or traffic-free commuting. Community schemes - ranging from simple tree-planting on the one hand, to the complete restoration of lost canals on the other - give locals a sense of pride and ownership in their canals. A wide range of educational initiatives encourage children to be the canal guardians of the next generation, be they simply dipping for subaquatic canal fauna or re-exploring life afloat aboard restored narrowboats like British Waterways'*Atlas* pictured elsewhere in this book.

The same canals which logistically-fuelled the region's meteoric rise to the 19th century status of 'workshop of the world' can now be seen to be entering a new golden era of tourism and heritage, providing recreational activities for all the family. The sheer sloth of water transport, which consigned it to commercial oblivion, is now, paradoxically, the most appealing aspect of the canals. In an age obsessed with time, or rather, the lack of it, the absence of speed inherent in any exploration of the canal system, has got to be a good thing. People have always respected the restorative powers of spring water - nowadays *canal* water can be just as beneficial too.

British Waterways

Mike Webb

Useful Contacts

Tourist Information Centres

Birmingham
2 City Arcade - Tel: 0121 643 2514
Victoria Square - Tel: 0121 693 6300
The Mall, ICC - Tel: 0121 665 6116
Central Library - Tel: 0121303 4511
Dudley
Churchill Centre - Tel: 01384 812830
Walsall
St Pauls Street - Tel: 01922 653110
Wolverhampton
Queen's Square - Tel: 01902 556110

Canals

British Waterways
Bayleys Lane, Tipton - Tel: 0121 506 1300
British Waterways are responsible for the care and maintenance of over 2,000 miles of canals and navigable rivers throughout the country. Their local office is at Ocker Hill at the junction of the Walsall and Tame Valley canals.

Boat Hire
If you've enjoyed your first contact with the canals of Birmingham and the Black Country you might be considering hiring your own narrow boat for a water-based exploration of the area. The following is a selection of companies offering boats for hire in the area - most boats are offered for hire on weekly terms.
Alvechurch Boat Centres - Tel: 0121 445 2909
Associated Cruisers - Tel: 01902 23673
Drifters - Tel: 0345 626252
Sherborne Wharf - Tel: 0121 455 6163
Water Travel - Tel: 01902 782371

Canal Societies
Two voluntary organisations , the Birmingham Canal Navigations Society and the Inland Waterways Association, foster interest in the canals covered by this book. Both welcome new members. Telephone the IWA head office on 01923 711114 for details of the current membership secretaries of both organisations.

Public Transport

Centro Hotline
Telephone 0121 200 2700 for details of all local bus and train services.

Further Reading

Magazines

Three monthly magazines devoted to inland waterways are currently available in High Street newsagents. These are:
Canalboat - Tel: 0118 977 1677
Canal & Riverboat - Tel: 01372 741411
Waterways World - Tel: 01283 742951

Books

Regretably, there are few books currently in print which do more than scratch the surface of the canals of Birmingham and the Black Country. There is no history of the BCN other than passing reference to it in standard works on inland waterways. A series entitled *The Industrial Canal* is setting out to cover the BCN in some detail. Published by the Heartland Press, 100 Frederick Road, Stetchford, Birmingham B33 8AE, the first volume, by Ray Shill, is devoted to coal; the second, by Tom Foxon, concerns the railway interchange trade. Two books published by M & M Baldwin, 24 High Street, Cleobury Mortimer, Kidderminster DY14 8BY give some idea of the atmosphere of the BCN in its final, post WWII years of commercial use. These are: *Bread Upon The Waters* by David Blagrove and *Anderton For Orders* by Tom Foxon.

Canal related titles aren't always easily obtainable from general booksellers, a fact which emphasises their perception as a minority interest. Perhaps the best choice of canal matter anywhere in the country is at the Canal Museum, Stoke Bruerne in Northamptonshire - Tel: 01604 862229. An alternative specialist retailer (of all transport related material) is: Midland Counties Publications, Maizefield, Hinckley, Leics. LE10 1YF. Tel: 01455 233747.